Verses Painted in Silence

Cassandra Napoli

DEDICATION

To those I have loved, hurt, mourned, and most importantly: to myself and those who are finding their voice.

ACKNOWLEDGMENTS

I'd like to thank the person holding this book and reading this page right now. Using writing as a conduit to express myself and spread kindness to those who are open to receiving it has been a goal of mine for years. I'm hoping that you'll be inspired within these pages, and maybe even motivated, to pick up a pen yourself and dabble in the importance of this particular form of storytelling. That is, of course, if you haven't done so before. I'd also like to thank myself for actually finishing this project and striving to get the passion for poetry out into the world again. I'm proud of you Cas, you've done something good here.

PREFACE

I wish to say that while yes, the premise of this book is to get you to adore poetry the way I do and feel inspired through my work, it isn't *solely* displaying such. The progression of me as a poet is also showcased within these pages, with the timeline stemming from the beginning of 2022 to mid 2023. That being said, there's a year and a half worth of my growth as a writer that's exhibited here! Some are written on the same day where I project how I was feeling, whereas others are simply concepts I came up with that I wanted to write about. This book also has various types of poetry. Some are in a modern format whereas others have a more complex structure to them. I preface all of this because there won't be a table of contents to get you to jump from what your heart desires; so read at your own pace and choose where you want to start!

Verses Painted in Silence

Cassandra Napoli

Life's tough. Everyone has their struggles, some worse than others. Hell, I'm sure everyone reading this right now is currently facing a battle or two. It doesn't matter what it may be that someone's going through. Whether it's minor or significant in your eyes, they're all traumatic events to the person. Despite all of us going through different scenarios, the aftermath results in us becoming mentally kindred. Life doesn't come with a manual on how to properly live because there isn't one right way. We aren't meant to be given the answers or else it'll just be too easy. Life's a learning experience and it is through those experiences and people you meet that'll put you in situations where you'll have to contend out of the dark. It is through the things you did to get yourself out of the dark, the lessons you've learnt from the mistakes both you and those around you have made, that'll allow you to pass it on to others in hopes to ease their pain. Life doesn't come with a manual because you are your own life's manual. No one else's, yours; and just like any given manual, you can read it as many times as you'd like, but you must fully analyze every depth of it to get a complete understanding of what to do. You must get an understanding of who you are before you can leap towards change.

The Question "Why don't I love myself? often stems from the fact that they don't love themselves the correct way. Some people refuse to verbalize their feelings, whether that's due to their experience attempting to in the past, not knowing how to word it properly, fear of being misunderstood, anything right? So for a lot of people, they've learnt to fend for themselves, and in doing so, they developed the other kind of love. The kind of love that solely appreciates themselves for the work they do rather than them as a whole. These are the people who choose to aid others by having them know they're understood and that they aren't alone in their thoughts. They do this because they know what it's like to not have someone there, to have to rely on themselves. When you only have that one way love that branches from just the ability to be comfortable alone, that tough love, you forget how to truly love yourself. You focus on giving that love that you've always craved for yourself to other people in hopes that no one has to go through it. I hope one day you'll be able to allow yourself to feel that kind of love from somebody else as that's the love you deserve.

Life is like watching the water droplets on your car
window during a rainy day.
Each drop competes its way to the bottom,
completely losing itself along the race.
As you grow, you learn to compare yourself to
everyone else
And in result, you unintentionally turn life into
a never ending track.
Life isn't a game that can be won, but to be
experienced
Stop focusing on the things that are
out of your control.

Some people feel that the past still has control over them. Those memories and those behaviors from the past hold messages about what's important to us in the present. They're a part of who we are, so if we get rid of them, we get rid of a piece of ourselves.

~ *Acceptance*

Sometimes the nights count longer than the days. When your eyes are shut for 8 hours straight, 6 feet under the anesthesia, yet your brain never stops spiraling; leaving you unable to scream.

Your mind is like a ticking time bomb. It has you playing hide and seek behind a smile, losing yourself whilst pretending and masking away as a preferred face. The temporary satisfaction of voices just out of reach beyond a screen, the hollowness of your smile which no longer beams. Aiding people in finding their path to the next chapter only because you want to be the set example of the person you needed during the times all was vacant. Where the words, "I'm not okay" feel as equivalent as lying under-oath.

I think people prefer me more when they know me less. It's easier to be the therapist than it is to be the client. With the days beginning to collide to one endless and suffocating loop, the words unable to escape its roots — where all is suppressed and can't seem to surface. Being around a diversity of voices and yet still alone, barely washed up on shore. Lungs giving out as you constantly redirect the tears all the way down. Where aiding people with their troubles has begun to feel like self-torment. Reminding others what you should be stating to yourself, slowly fading into the nothingness of its excruciating cycle. I used to ask myself, "Why do you care about people?" And to that I'd answer for the sole reason of understanding. The closure after learning one's story and how that had an impact on their future days can sometimes help you in a way. It never really helped me as it did them though, and maybe it's due to a further reason which is that not many people are able to express their love towards others. The world's cold like that, but now it's begun to trap me. Like I'm enclosed in a room that theoretically I could get out of, yet my brain has created the illusion of the locked door and how the sun burns like fire if you were to make contact with it. I despise being on the receiving end, but I'm becoming deranged. The boiling anger that's as hot as the flames of the sun, and the emptiness that's as dull as the vacant room I'm in. I guess it's funny how people only truly express that they care once you've benefited them. Once you took the time to accommodate for them in their time of need. They only seek your presence when they need something of you. Or when you're in so much pain that it's that noticeable that they reach out. I can't seem to tell who's friend and who's foe anymore. Everyone in my surroundings is beginning to drain me. It's as though I'm a puppet with an abusive puppeteer, constantly being passed onto the next person to love unconditionally, never receiving it back. Love is meant to be fulfilling, so why do I feel as though I'm a ghost when it comes to those within that category? Perhaps I should stop caring all together. Give in to the taunting thoughts that have been nagging at me to let out that anger. To become the past version of myself that was buried for what appears to be decades ago. Its seems that I'm at war with myself again, and I'm afraid I won't conclude in a victory this time. This appears to be one of the longer chapters of my life's book, but like previous ones such as this, my character always remained in tact in the next. So I can repeat history in that sense, I hope.

Sometimes I wish I was a goldfish inside its bowl. Displayed for anyone to see, unable to reach unless you dive deep. How can one ever know peace when all they do is throw away their heart for anyone to find? For this heart isn't bland, it's special; it's one of a kind. So why wouldn't anyone want it barricaded behind a dome? If only there were a lock and key, otherwise no one would enter for free. But if they don't have to pay to enter your heart, why do they only appreciate you once you're gone? Maybe it's because you made it easy. You loved them and expressed it effortlessly that they didn't feel like they needed to put any time into you. Maybe it's because they were secretly guilty. Guilty of not being able to produce the love you do, let alone understand how, so they end up distancing themselves altogether. Or maybe, just maybe, they never loved you to begin with.

The kindest people aren't always born that way. They were mended into that image. They are the ones that had been casted aside and shut out, preventing themselves from ever feeling a sense of belonging. As if they couldn't be understood. They are the ones who faced all their demons without a shoulder to rest on. The ones who never dared to ask for help. Courtesy of suppressing their emotions, bottling it all up, is that eventually that sadness turned into anger. Whether they meant it to or not, that anger ended up inflicting others. Guilt began to strike. They are the ones who dug themselves out of the dark, and in doing so, were left with a permanent scar from the damage they had caused. Now, they choose to strive towards helping everyone around them as a way to understand themselves. Even though they put on a tough act, those demons haven't been demolished. They're still in there, lurking, scraping against their soul trying to find a way to be released again. This is a reminder that even the kindest people have their struggles. So please, check up on the person that seems to be there for everyone. Check up on your family, your friends, heck even your pet if you have one. But most importantly, check up on yourself, because you are that kindest person. You deserve your love. You deserve all of the love that you give to others. Never forget that.

You can live without them. You can get out of bed without their scent dispersed throughout your room. You can have a productive day without receiving a message or call from them. You can survive without their guidance because you did just that before they entered your life. We are all born as warriors, and although we are surrounded by a diversity of faces, we start out alone. Brought into a world that's of nothing but chaos, yet we can make something good out of it if we wish to. You're stronger than you can ever conceive, you survived this long when all the colors were black. When all hope was lost. When you were astray in your own subconscious without a sight of a hand to catch you from falling deeper into your cavernous mind. You pulled yourself out of the dark, you found the light. Be proud of how you've managed to persevere, even when the odds weren't in your favor. Appreciate yourself for the effort you've taken to get here. Acknowledge how courageous you are for conquering your demons. If you happen to have met some folks along the journey back to yourself then that's an extra bonus. It's important to have individuals in your surroundings that love you, but if you ever find yourself questioning it or things heading south, know that you can go on without them. It won't be easy, but missing them is a part of the process, and you'll get to head on a new journey. One where you'll meet others who won't ever make you doubt their fondness of you. Ones who won't disappear, because you deserve those kind of people in your life. So breathe. It's okay to feel stuck without them. It's okay to struggle. Just know that this isn't the end. You are the star to your life, and although you may be sitting on the sidelines right now, the sun will make its way over to you. It just takes time for things to align and retain orbit. Your happiness will return, and when it does, you'll have gratitude for enduring everything that came your way to get there, I promise.

I know all you may want to do is throw yourself off the nearest exit. To give in to the intrusive thoughts lurking in the shadows within your mind and the ghosts in the midst of those roaming around you. I know you think this world has nothing left to offer, and you're right. The world has absolutely nothing to give, but you do. You have yet to even fathom the essence you trail behind you. The potential you have in positively impacting this generation. The gift you bare in shedding some light into what feels like an endless abyss. You may think you take up too much space, but I think you've yet to reach even a quarter of where you'll go. The people you'll spark. The souls you'll touch. The difference you'll make. What you're doing now. You have yet to realize just how special of an individual you are. With a smile that can end a war, and a fear that may call upon your door, you have the heart of a dozen nations, my friend. You will wake up tomorrow because you have sailed harsher waves than this. You will wake up tomorrow because you are so much more than what you claim to be. You will wake up tomorrow because I'm here to reiterate how much I love you. How much your presence alone brightens my day. How you simply existing is enough for me. I want to hear about your story, not have to tell it; because you are someone worth knowing and someone who is worth every sacrifice. You will wake up tomorrow because it's today that is bad, not tomorrow. Not life. Not the further days you have. No no, there are still so many moments that you have yet to experience yet, so be ready for them. Because although you may feel empty now, when that ray of light comes your way, it'll be an overwhelming amount of joy, but it's worth every ounce. You deserve the comfort that you inflict on those around you, so allow me to remind you that it's okay to feel the way you're feeling. Its okay to not be okay. It's okay to need a break. It's okay to sit and ponder about the world for all the harm that's been inflicted into your life, because it shows that you know what you yearn for. Life may be short, yet the patience needed can be excruciating, I know. But enjoy the ride, because sometimes all it takes is a few wrong turns and bumpy roads to finally lead you to your destination. The location that you were meant to be led to this whole time. So please, don't give up.

Even though you may not be able to love yourself, you deserve to feel and be loved by those around you. You deserve to wake up in the morning and head into the parlor to people with grins on their faces the second they see you've entered the room. You deserve to feel safe when it comes to opening up about any disputes that have happened in your life. You deserve to feel understood, to be heard. To have a sense of purpose. You don't deserve to wake up in the morning with singular convictions of — Why am I still alive? Why am I not loved? Why am I not enough? You aren't meant to go through such hostilities alone. You don't deserve to feel like a waste of space. **You** deserve to live, and I mean *truly* live. To run along the most beautiful fields with the sun in pursuit whilst setting into an exquisite orange hue, only to watch it set and be driven out by the moonlight, who glistens over the ceaseless lake that's in front of your gaze. To live as if it was your last without a doubt in mind. To obtain the knowledge that you are capable of changing this world. You may not love yourself just yet, but trust in the people who do. For they see the you that you have yet to even fathom, the one who will take your very own breath away.

There is nothing wrong with being sensitive. In a world that has grown cold and running on its few remaining embers, it is completely understandable as to why you may feel out of place. But you aren't. You are just as deserving to be here as anyone else is. Being sensitive means that you experience life at a higher frequency than others, and there is absolutely nothing wrong with that. If anything, it allows you to establish what type of people you prefer around you, and also your general wants and needs. That truth can be difficult to conclude on because sometimes we need comfort that is not commonly sought out, but never mistaken that as you asking for too much. When it comes to your mental health, it is never too much to ask for help.

You're not a burden or too much despite being in a negative place. You're a human being. You're allowed to have feelings, and you're allowed to not be okay. We're meant to go through the horrors of our life to be able to comprehend our interpretation of happiness. Without that guidance, that pain, we wouldn't be able to decipher between the light and the dark. We'd just have that observant attribute that in light we can see, whereas in darkness we can't. These substandard eras of our lives are essential so we are able to analyze how certain situations effect us. They allow us to evaluate our environment and construct a narrative as to why it's making us feel the way they do, and what we can execute to change that. So no, you're not a burden for being in a negative place, you're simply being human; and that is all that can ever be asked of you.

One of the hardest things to do is to turn the page when you know that person isn't going to be in the next chapter. But you need to. Some people are in your life temporarily, well technically everyone in your life is, but that's not the point. You will meet people that you envision your future with, but the devastating truth is that you don't know what holds for you in the future. Sure, you can hope and dream, but that doesn't assure anything. Rather than trying to hold a grudge or find a reason to hate someone for leaving, take it as a lesson. Despite how awful someone is to you, it's all about how you respond. Every person you meet will teach you something. You learn what not to do, what to do. What signs to look for early on so you don't put yourself in a similar situation again. Never regret anything that's happened in your life. Never regret the people you've met. It can't be undone nor forgotten, and no matter how hard you try to, you'll end up dwelling on it more. It's time you start focusing on the lessons behind what someone taught you so that it'll keep you content in the now.

You're going to be okay. Now I know that doesn't mean a hell of a lot right now, but you need to give yourself more credit. Despite all you've gone through, all of the moments where life has barricaded you into what feels like the cavernous depths of an endless void: You're still here. When the odds weren't in your favor, you rose and fought back with all you had and came out victorious. They say no side ever wins during war, which has truth to it, but just celebrate on surviving another day. For there were several casualties on either side, yet both had to be severed from you. For they were the sacrifice needed to allow you to bloom into the individual you truly are. So if you can't get yourself out of bed today then that's absolutely okay. Productivity is not the key to your self-worth, it's all about evaluating your current state, processing how it was established, how it's making you feel in the present moment, and what you can do to slowly reverse it. That takes time, so don't be so harsh on yourself if you weren't able to go on that cycle ride you wanted to do, or that party you were invited to. You're in the aftermath of a war, and even after winning, there's still a recovery process. So be patient with yourself and know that you will overcome this. You will be okay.

The hero is almost always orphaned in some aspect. The villain, if you observe carefully, has either a scar, a limp, some sort of speech impediment; something that makes them stand out. What that indicates is that this person had a painful past. A mark that was seared into the image they're now perceived to be. So the real difference between the protagonist and antagonist is simply how they respond to pain. The hero says, "The world hurt me, so I'm not going to let it hurt anyone else." Whereas the villain says, "The world hurt me, so I'm going to hurt it back."

It's not that you don't love yourself, no. You just don't love what has been instilled not to love. Your thoughts are being taunted with. You see as a kid, you were full of light — there was no such thing as darkness, except the nights in which you spent being mesmerized by the moon. As you got older, however, reality hit, but your happiness as a child didn't have to go away, we've just made it so.

It's through every thought that you keep lingering inside that every decade goes by. Where your memories begin to fade as your dreads get pushed farther and farther away. I know life is tough, we face obstacles that no one should have to endure, and that may leave you in dark thoughts at times. Though please remember that at the death of dark arises dawn, and at the bed of today lies a new tomorrow.

Even though there is not much hope left to believe it, there is a light at the end of the tunnel, I promise you. Even when there's only a few embers left, just one spark could ignite the flames it needed to bloom. Sometimes you have to go through hardships to conquer yourself. Sometimes it is through the nights overweighing the days that allow you to properly gaze at the stars and feel the serenity in the accomplishment of just being here today.

Do you ever look in the mirror and something stares back at you, but it isn't yourself?

It's a non-recognizable phenomenon; an indistinguishable shadow that casts behind you and never vacates from your side, your mind. Who's always attached to you and has barricaded themselves into the depths of your soul; becoming a symbol of your darkness.

And so wherever you go, it'll follow — so long as a ray of light is existent. Being a constant reminder that you're carrying a weight. One that in time will disfigure you.

However, whether you allow that gloom to take control or not will be the initiation of a new beginning.

A commemoration honoring one's self for the demons that have been demolished, or become petrified as the fiend emerges from the cavernous pit and takes the steering well; branding you the puppet with a drunken puppeteer — unable to differentiate friend and foe, thus losing yourself entirely.

It's the moment of your voice longing to be heard, yet unable to produce a word. Obtaining the intrusive thoughts of being a monstrosity; abstracts instilled within your mind that progressively make you evade the identity of who you are. When you've portrayed yourself to be the villain, someone who's believed to have caused so much destruction around them — leaving the only liable option to sever them from this world. A process in which leaves you in a constant state of psychosis, fabricating illusions that are unable to be depicted, causing you to altercate and never feel understood by anyone; especially yourself. Concocting a story in which paints you as a perpetrator. One who's loathed and forsaken by those around them, gradually losing their morality as they become the character they feared they'd become all along. But the only real difference between a hero and a villain is just who's telling the story.

It sucks when all you want to do is release the weight that you're carrying to anyone other than the people you create within your mind. Someone real. Someone to prove that there are still good people left in this god-for-saken world. That your made up character's personalities can be seen in others too. But that thought is also an illusion. To open your phone only to realize that no one's there, because that's *your* job, right? **You're** meant to be the messenger. The <u>provider</u>. The <u>wise</u>. They don't care about you. They only care for what they can take from you. It's only when that sadness turns into anger that they care. It's only until that bubbly person they once knew fades away that they'll listen. They just express their affection once it's too late. They only love the good sides to you, the bad isn't worth knowing as it doesn't benefit them, right? No one cares when you cry, they're only there when you smile. Because while they were seeing a brightly lit individual who aided them through everything, you were at war with your own mind. You've learned to hide away from the source of your suffering by healing those around you. A damaging mechanism that only seeks to increase in its severity.

You never know what someone's going through behind the mask they wear, so ask a loved one how they're doing today. Ask a friend. A stranger. Yourself. Anyone. Don't hold back when it comes to expressing how you feel because ultimately, you never know when you'll lose that opportunity to. So just say what's on your mind. Tell your family, your friends, your neighbors that you care about them. But don't just say it, actually put some effort behind it because we all know actions speak louder than words.

Time is never existent with you. You were the sun to my moon; the light to my darkness. Such opposites, yet correlate and attract in synonymous ways. Because for what seemed like minutes was hours, and what appeared to be hours became days. We don't even need to talk, just the silence: Being in your presence fills a void in my heart that I can't even fathom.

A version of me died the day I found you, but it also forged the me that I'm slowly learning to understand. You are the reason for the death of a person who wasn't able to love, let alone feel loved. Thank you for not counting the dials on the clock waiting for time to pass by. Thank you for not only being infatuated by my existence, but for also attempting to resurrect the apparition of me that I never knew I still needed. Thank you for reminding me of the stars that glimmer around and resemble me, even at my worst.

The first poem I ever wrote was 3 words long.
One that contained minimal dialect, yet expressed a pictorial
narrative.

Words that ended wars amongst the unknown.
Seized the light in depths of darkness.
Opening my eyes to a new outlook on life.

That's when you know you've reached a certain state.
When you care for something so much to the point of
not caring at all.
Growing to understand that it was only ever you that
had fabrications of the future — the other in the past.
Questioning the status of your story, coming to terms with
the fact that the stars amongst the night sky replace each other.

Those 3 words that had originated from a place of love
are now replaced with another 3 worded poem.
One that is not represented as an individual star, but an entire
constellation of yearning, yet also grievance.

~ *I hate you.*

The earth stays at a distance,
Never daring to move closer,
Yet continues to orbit the sun.
It clings onto a hope.
One that narrates an ideal pair,
Yet understanding it'll never end up just them two.
For the moon,
Despite being tens of millions of miles away,
Is far more feasible to the sun.
Which is why the earth has little to no appreciation toward the stars;
All they've ever represented were elements of what could've been.
The earth is synonymous to the moon in many ways.
They can never be still,
Thus meaning they'll never collide with one another
The annihilation of a utopian galaxy,
And the confirmation that it was just a longing toward false hope.

I Look To The Sky

I look to the sky when I've had a bad day
The clouds never seem to be far away
And just as the clouds, they're a temporary anguish
For in time they shall all be vanquished

And though a rainy day is nothing more than a drought
Its assets leave you an abundance of doubt
As hostilities worsen, you'll wish to flee
But never forget the importance of its debris

These negative thoughts will tempt you in ways
In which its sequel consists of a hefty maze
The commencing of learning these thoughts had to amass
For in time they shall all surpass

And so I look to the sky once my days have brightened
Only to observe that I've been enlightened
One's demons were demolished, yet will return
Though never forget this is to yearn

The Unwanted Child

They sat perched beside the campfire,
roasting marshmallows and toasting to jubilations and prayers.
Listening to the distinct laughter of the other children just by
the stream;
hoping that by tossing pebbles into the abysmal depths of the
water,
they'd aid in drowning out the wailing silhouettes that lingered
just beyond the horizon.

A darkness that happened to be the most present in daylight.
One that tainted the depiction of themself and the scenery
around them,
thus not feeling any ounce of belonging.
There had to be an antidote to this suffering.
For the declaration of their triumph only came with the initial
depth of their despair.

Can you be both a miracle and mistake at the same time?
A soul that had flourished into this world with glee, yet
a constant reminder that they don't equate with thee.
Commemorating a time in which they obtained value and
purpose; a time in which they were happy.
As now despite being physically seen, they were simply an
apparition waiting to be taken away.

And so they were, though it was not as it seemed.
For they were stripped of all they owned,
bested by those they knew as friends yet now were foes.
All they ever wanted was to be apart of something again.
To share a moment of pride without the feeling of it being a
goodbye.
The yearning for relishing each day as if it were the last,
instead of praying to be conquered by their past.

They were known as the child who burnt their village to the
ground. Though not because they had hatred toward their old
companions, no. They just wanted to feel the warmth of home
again.

At first I hated your company, so much so that I went blind. I could only ever see when one was stood in front of a light, but I could always decipher you from a crowd. I questioned what I'd done to deserve such a fiend, but despite the toxicity you've inherited onto me, you were my best friend. You knew me from the inside out. Never daring to lie, and always knowing when to pry. You're the reason I wore my headphones with one side out my ear. Why I doubted the people around me, or why I wished to no longer exist. You ruined my life, and yet I loved you. You understood me, you felt my pain. You embraced me. You never left me, even when all the colors were black. When shadows casted in the midst of an alleyway, the moonlight you radiated was used as the light to reveal the path ahead. Your voice, continuously lingering at the back of my mind. You made me feel less deranged, and yet I stared at you every morning with revulsion and sorrow. Every time I heard you I wanted to tear my tongue out. Anything you ate simply tasted like giving up. I don't know why I was so fixated and enraged by you at the same time, I couldn't seem to make up my mind. Perhaps deep down I wished to accept you just as I did with everyone else in my life, but you have done the most damage; considering the fiend you were was me. Learning to un-love you wasn't the hardest part, it was having to replace that void with a restructured version of myself. One that obtains the ability to surpass all wrong doings without a tainted view in scenery. I forgive you, but most importantly, I thank you. Thank you for teaching me how important it is to prioritize myself. Thank you for displaying how important it is to not be hard on myself, to not shy away from my problems by helping everyone else. Thank you for opening my eyes again: Allowing me to not just see color, but a whole new narrative on life.

I Am Proud of You

I am proud of you for not killing yourself today, for not giving up when the world has thrusted nothing but hardship overseas. Having to wake up everyday yet wishing that you hadn't, always asleep as it's a metaphoric and temporary death but also the devils advocate, is a difficult state of mind to conquer. When labeled as lazy or futile by those around you without them knowing you're in a spiritual warfare, taking your battle scars and inspiring others to admire their own — that is an individual with a yielded heart.

So in case no one has articulated this to you today, you need to give yourself more credit. You're worth more than any treasure in this world. You've inherited a warriors heart: One that undergoes several battles and concludes in countless casualties, yet never falters. I hope you know that it's okay to not be okay. You're allowed to savor the minuscule things that bring you joy, you're allowed to weep and mope about the hostilities that have sailed your way. There is no weakness in that, only strength.

I want you to know you are not alone. In times where your mind is clouded with judgement, your vision will be too foggy to see a clear viewpoint, but there are those around you that cherish your presence. I can absolutely promise you that. Because you're someone that is worth knowing, you are someone that is capable of obtaining the feeling of being loved.

I want you to be reminded that you are where you need to be, and while it may not be a desirable destination, do not rush the things you want most — you'll end up skimming past the journey itself which is what produces the moments containing your growth. Because although you may not be where you want to be yet, and while you may not think you have the ability to overcome this, you aren't where you used to be either; and that alone is absolutely beautiful.

Yin-Yang

The sun could hardly decipher their mistress, apart from knowing its kindred. Hundreds of gatherers glimmering through the most ruinous of days, a reminder that there shall always be light even in the interventions of rapture. Pivoting opposites, yet attract in the midst of rivalry.

A snake grovels toward its prey, confining them in what is synonymous to paralysis. Nearly winded, mind clouded, body trembling; though unable to act upon it. As if just their presence alone perforated its victim with a sword. Compelled to return to a state of tribulation, tangled along deceiving vines that began securing a padlock around one's windpipe, though the target was able to sever the link between both the fiend and its venomous tongue; bestowing triumph for one's acts of valor.

The sky and its clouds were aquatinted with one another, providing both guidance and wisdom. Blooming through the brilliance of the other; thus inspiring those near that had begun to peer. With the winds harmonizing flocks of birds just afar, singing melodies that signified tranquility yet also solitude. For the birds had no trees to perch on, nor commemoration of their effortless talents. The winds frolicked along forbidden skies whilst awaiting the fabrication of a hurricane; so they may use Mother Nature as an excuse to cause mischief, and leaving those receptive to become incongruous.

The sky and its clouds are acquainted with one another, yet they form an eclipse — one that forbids themselves from embarking the formation of a constellation. Which is why the sun can gape at stars and the moon can gaze at clouds. Why the snake can admire one who wields a sword, yet is also respected of their venom that punctures the silver-lining of stories aboard. In light there is dark, and in gloom there is gleam. Blasphemy is they who garners the thorn prior its rose.

There are times where you'll feel like that character in a scene. One who has a vast amount of people around them, yet the camera blurs them out. You can vaguely hear the music in the background, perceiving those conversing amongst one another, though it is all unclear. Almost as if rather than living, you're just existing. Existing for others contentment. Which is why the drugs and opinions you've forced into your body only provide an increase of the amount of thoughts that contain the involvement of giving up. Feeling vacant when your occupation is to simply please your peers, in hopes that it'll be rewarded by fixing yourself, though it never is. And with absorbing everyone else's emotions, you lose sight of your own. You may think you're only existing rather than living, but in reality, it's because of your clouded judgement that's been obtained due to your priorities on others and not yourself. You're the only one that's been paying attention; hence why everyone else is blurred. Your mind is trying to temporarily dispose those around you so it can attend to itself for once.

Heaven's Silence and Forsaken Hope

Have you misplaced your compassion toward me, oh *Heavenly Mother?*
Or was it the fragrance of my failures that drove you away?
The peacefulness in today felt dull beside chaos, who had yet begun
to chime in with the breeze and its current.

Though one mustn't forget the ecstasy of skewing off the roads of
those designed to be a gateway.
Discovering forbidden meadows within the silhouettes of its soil,
entranced by roots of solidity; containing both lock and key.

Oh how I miss your intrepid tongue, Heavenly Father.
As your aroma only ever signified triumph — even in the depths
of all despair.

Stranded with casualties of victory
Submerged in the dullness of rapture
Gasping breath as expense for fallen wings
The sun ascends along angels amongst the sky

Breathe and out you blow a cloud
Its droplets prevail, the current devours
An anchor secured the ship in its bottle
Sealed away sailing toward a false abode

Reap the sap of a willow tree's sorrows
For it cries vigorously
Competing with the winds
Who howl louder than the wolves
In the midst of daylight

Return the seedling to its soil
Relieve the pains of the sprout
Water over the deceptions and quarrels
Amongst its embedded roots
And flourish a sapless yet unhallowed woodland

They were led to a doorway
Revealing a tainted heart
Through the grief of sobriety

A lack of remorse had been present
Indulging the fragrance of blasphemy
A body that had no lock for you to put in a key

Blessed is the smile behind the frown
Teary eyes eroded by a singular blink
Transporting your sorrows to the pillow
Inducing a fleeting escape from its weight

Spare the silhouette who sought
out its own reflection
Unraveling a world from its
mirrored image
Though deceitful for yearning heaven
Thus the underlying traumas of oblation

I am rid of caring for those who ceased
to nurture me as I do them.
Who speak to me of apologies,
yet sorrows are all thats remained to be drowned out,
though may never be done.
False hope is what has become of me this.

A liability with a fractured heart,
Who craves the earth's
warmth in her palms.
With aspirations to venture
the world accompanied by one
defined neither friend or foe.

To embark on road trips, far from home.
The tranquility of the unknown consuming me.
It is such dainty things that
commence my curiosity for the wonders of this world.

I am not fractured: I am pure.
I've been misplaced in a generation where my
tastes of life get swallowed by my own tongue.
Where beauty of sensitivity has been severed
from representational art.
Words on a page simply a dialect rather than solace.
Though one shall only be tainted in such a way when
The observer becomes the reflector.

It's human nature to always want more, however, it doesn't mean that's the right way to live. When you can learn to not care if you lose everything, to not care what happens, you are truly living. You see in life, nothing is quite ours. We borrow it until we die, and onward it goes. It gets passed onto someone else, or blown around to frolic with the wind. Everything is the earth's. The only thing we truly own is the moments that we choose to experience.

The birds were indebted to you
Caroling melodies of lands far amble than this one
Fixated by the discomfort of the nest
The flock had no choice but to flee
Manufacturing wings of tears and faltered dreams

Mystic Invitation

I miss the resonance of bliss
When stars shared
the warmth of the sun
Though the moon its fuse

Draping vines, a toast to droughts
Sunken bubbled ships along the oceans blaze
Tangling riverbeds acquaint
the frigid stone wall

A drawbridge to our gateway
The treasure map of a maze
Bestowing one's secrets
In the barrels of treachery

Join us, dear friend
Unhinge from the lonesome
Drown your tales of woe
And be gone the wails

Young yet shriveled
Though greener the sod decays
Weaved droplets of aid traveled the roots
Seeking refuge in its kindred
The density consumed them
As waves with its sadistic current

They've since returned to clouds amongst the timid sky
Drenched in the absorption of primordial oceans
Anguished shall be a tempest for decades
Being rid the weights of overseas
Washed ashore indistinctive winds
Awaiting obscurity of the droplets reminisce

There is courage in tenuous stems
Amongst the recipient of one's cruelty
I am no hero, though a chevalier

Browse for a hex
Ridicule my injustice for power
Unravel wilted petals sifting a flourished heart

Fields of gold
It's weighted cavalry
The fatality of luxury, worshipped at my alter

And play me a lullaby one last time
Each strum a buoyant breeze
Consecrate my remains to the earth

Bestow the prominence of peace

Coldness of the bathroom floor
Water seeps through its frothed secrets
An absence of serotonin, the antidote
Numbness called upon another day

My canvas, my target; my heart
Streaks of paint were shed
Splattering ink amongst an arrowhead
Delivering frailty on a platter

Pains of today have been stroked away
Its hue's residue yet remains
The fixation of silver-linings sedate me
Synchronizing the affliction of withdrawal

A sadistic brush sourced my breathless lungs
Its dyed waters eradicating all sanity
Thus one was declared another visit
Though I can never escape

The reason we close our eyes
When suffering hardship,
When we sleep or kiss
Is because the most beautiful
Things and pains in life are felt by the heart

And I find that absolutely breathtaking
To be in front of someone you love,
Going on a holiday and admiring the scenery
That encompasses you;
Its not about what you see
It's about how it makes you feel

And while you wish to not close your eyes
To block out its presence, you do anyway
Though not of fear, no,
But out of acceptance
You're indulging the air of the atmosphere that
Flows through your lungs
Knowing it'll all be there when opening your
Eyes once again,
That it's not fiction this time
And you feel more joyful
Each moment you have a prolonged blink
With your eyes

That right there contains the precious aspects of life

I ponder you quite often
I'm classified as your personalized database
And at first I wore it honorably
Discreetly fond of bestowing such a status
A superior of those who've known you prior

My moments shared with you have been remorseless
3600 ticks of the clock for every hour that has gone by
And oh, how I could compile memoirs that date back
Centuries to our initial encounter
Yet sometimes departure is a necessary plight

There was no pleasure retaining such a title
For its healing amongst my anguish became temporary
Reminiscing folk tales conceived to lose track of time
And though its been 10 months since I've sailed home
I've been hypothermic upon my arrival

And so I thank you one last time
For your aid in my safety from currents and its waves
Drowning out the screeches that lurked within my mind
You will forever be my precious cargo
Cruising beyond the waters horizon with the shore just out of
reach

I hereby set you free, my friend
For it is time I let you go
And should we find each other in another lifetime
I will welcome you with open arms
Though until then. . .

. . .May we meet again

The Remaining Flower

The remaining flower has begun to wilt
As I stand the coronation of its thorns
Recalling those who came before
Laughter a faint memory
Joy found through suffering

Fallen comrades flourish
Echos festering at wounds
Taunting your every move
Like if you aren't physically ill
Then must you be a sinner

Oh, to be a young girl once again
Innocence galore,
Never awaiting demons on
The other side of your door
Hiding from the cruelties of this world

Though now comforted by its presence
Indebted to their fellowship
And as ones idle for a suicide commences
The last petal has detached
Thus you are free, you may prosper

My Daunting Conscious

There is a voice in my head
That says,
"I forsake you from
Retaining calming waters, for I
Have undergone the suffrage of
Its stillness."
And my mind flares for aid,
Unable to stabilize the waves.
All the while, a looming
Figure is persistent.
With a stare that
Breaths my beat-less heart,
There is an adolescent
Angst of being torn apart.
It taunts and it vexes,
Procuring control over
My mangled vessel.
Sealing me away in preparation
For a battle.
A noose throttles
The roots of my eyes,
As I am to witness the destruction
Through its lenses:
Overtaking the feebler
In order to win the war.
Though hostilities are not to be won,
There to be endured.
The casualties of today
Sought the refuge of tomorrow.
The absence of triumph
Spark the unexpected light.
There is beauty in the grit of
The fragile fighter.
For they are often those
Who have foreseen the most.
They just so happened to have
Vitalized internally,
Long enough for them to secure
Their demons from grasping the

Stems of the world
Like the roots of their eyes.
Thus too, they are victorious.
They have prevailed.

In The Name of The Well

And now we have reached the most difficult part
When wishing wells - no longer a conduit for our stability
Where our affirmations to each other froth up and foam white lies
Making all you want to do being blending your fist with the brick
wall that you always have on standby
When you can no longer keep up with counting the days
Where the sun has perforated your vision with their temptations in
trusting its light
Who knew folklore of sacred ground that primarily granted us
hope would be the destination of our plight?
For when the sun glazes over the well, it masks its blasphemous
waters
Securing a place on our soil with its cavernous tunnel
Where its inhabitants perpetually flow through the wails of our
drought
Where much like 2 sides of a coin: we are forged together, though
never able to face one another
Thus tossing ourselves into the void was never meant to be a
triumph, for we have drained the well of its nature
And now we have reached the end of this tale
All in the name of the well

Eternal Tides: A Sunlit Odyssey

Tread lightly on the path to the sun
For there is still mending to be done
We've built a foundation on grains of sand
Not knowing the idle of its land
And when the oceans divided, we're left in drought
Unable to retain, thus obtaining doubt

Our land no longer feasible, the ship has set sailed
As we yearn for the wind to afloat and prevail
Though we rest on separate waters, its currents intertwined
Easing our worries of not being aligned

For the sun awaits the moon on commemorating its light
Just so it can rest and reciprocate its plight
And though they can never collide or interface with one another
It's their reflections on the ocean that instill they're ones lover

The Lighthouse

Oh dear lighthouse,
I yearn to have sought my anchor prior to our ships arrival
For the entrancement of your glare was that of a vigorous stare
Our captain, dismissing my curiosities of your beauty
Producing one's lust at the solitude of your reservedness

To think how you've been alone upon meeting us, yet surrounded
by the wails of waves in which long to devour you
Tell me, did my love for you create the padlock which now
prevents the beams of your bright white hue?
Is that why I no longer see beyond your view?

I accompanied you *four* weeks, though persistently out of arms
reach
For the nights had prolonged the days
As an extension of figments brought malaise
And I'd begun to ponder, what bestowed me to endure the
torments of wanting to discover?

Because when drawn to you, I look to the moon's glaze
For it contains a similar hope which you unknowingly phrase
And without you, dear light, I fear to be submerged by the oceans
appetite
But I too have been starved before the storm, scavenging the
remains of my past reform

Though it was I who emerged the sadistic waters
For it was said to allude my mind's scoffers
And I'm sorry, beloved Captain, but you have caused this of me
You ridiculed my compliance, which has since converted to
defiance

I know not of what to do to retain the last droplets of my sanity
For there is no longer the light, nor the voice which held me tight
And the moon, who once comforted me dear, has ceased to appear
Keeping me up all night in hopes that you're near

Oh lighthouse,
I yearn the fixations of you be reserved for my death bed

For the Captain's chair now evicted due my desire in striking him dead
My entrancement for your embrace has costed my sobriety
And vexing my anchor which had once confided in me

Threads of Redemption: Penance and Desire

Why must I, a treacher, pardon the sins of another?
Would that not be my ailment, dear *Mother*?
For the depictions of my plight are caused by the reveries of one's might
Though is this to be my downfall, my spite?

Oh, how I long for your reflection despite my affliction
Though drowning out the truth, of course,
Blending its frothed waters to align with the night sky's youth
What has become of me this?
For I long the resonance of bliss in which that I dearly miss

And where are you, my dear *Sun*?
What has the wretch in which they call *The Moon* done?
For your absence aroused my desire in perpetrating shooting stars
Yet blinded by the reverence in its foreseeable scars

Oh, will you ever return to me, my dear friend?
As I wish to put this longing of you to bed
For of that we are, kindred silhouettes
Who frolic to the winds' deceitful regrets
And I toast to our love, for it holds me bare
Though it punctures my lungs as I'm smothered by your tongue

But why must I, a misunderstood, strike the hands of another?
Would that not be wrong of me, dear *Mother*?
For the endurance of life brought grievance to all which was bright
Though is this to be my repentance, retrieving the light?

Eidolon

I've never truly encountered
your presence
Though your silhouette
glistens through the rays of
tainted eyes with its darkness
The more my vision adjusts
to your light
The prone you are to
corrupt in its trite

For I relish your spirit
As I'm aware you're not there
Yet I'm the director
of your picture
Therefore you're
prized my vigor
And when you
vanquish yourself to sober me
It evokes why I doubt

So now I can't help but ponder,
Are you just another lesson that
awaits to be overridden?
An apparition claiming
to be your candid face?
God, I miss when your
voice was my embrace

Though it does beg the question,
What returns you to
the humble abode
that is my head?
For what you were,
solely the fragrance of
my minds high
And when you arise,
I hear the whispers alluding your figure
As it replenishes my dismay of you,
dear oppressor

But why are you not who
I know you to be?
For I wouldn't dread at your grave
Bargaining to be in your place
If I'd of known I was the only one
to attend your wake
And yet still, I grieve you
So shall I wager my 6 feet for yours?
Or wonder if your haunting
is to be allured?

Elegy of Silent Law

In times of war, the law falls silent
Just as leaves when the sun begins to migrate
For we confine our breaths with the sword of tongue
And await to bask in the piles of our young

The caskets of triumph roam the streetlights of heart
And fear our fondness in coveting their depart
For the heads we grieve toward are the ones we turn on
Just as they who suffer the sins of a sole pawn

And they speak of those sins through the fumes of their remains
Bestowing our rivals with what we *too* endure with haze
Though how long 'till we see the sun again, will that day even
come?
Or must we resume our sulking in what cannot be done?

Sun-Kissed Love

I just want you to know that when I think of you
I think of the sun
For its beams of light arise
No matter the storm in sight
And you absorb my drought with your presence
Evaporating the riverbeds in which we've bled
Therefore I no longer fear the moon's arrival
For you outshine any of its stars
As you waver the sky in my arms
And your reflection on my waters
Reminds why the current keeps you afloat
For you've rekindled my spirit
Allowing me the embrace of your love
And with you, darling,
I feel as though even the void couldn't devour us
For the clouds are at our beckon call
To aid us during the times we fall
Just as you with me when scared and wish to flee
I just want you to know that when I think of you
I think of the sun
For it's what my eyes fancy upon waking up
And though it used to be a dread for each day
It's now a conduit that yearns for today to obey
As now I would cast a shadow on the world
If it meant I'd get to savor in your words

Chasing Moonlight

I fancy running away from daytime
Though I'm not sure why
Perhaps I fond the stillness of the night
For there is never one like me in sight
Not that there ever is, anyway
Or maybe
I simply dislike the brightness up close
For I gaze at the moon and its stars the most
The farther away it is, the more at home I feel
And I admire all that be covered in dew
As I quench my thirst in attempts to subdue
Though I yearn for the cold sand
To mold into glass
May it sculpt my desired reflection
As it shatters my current objection
For the solace found through hardship
Corrupts the conjurings of my dreams
And when I seek for the oceans aid
I'm obscured by its frothed neglect
Though once being exiled for quite some time
I would very much like to return to the light
This unfamiliarity brings comfort in my mist
Yet the warmth which trembled my heart,
I do dearly miss
And despite the ailment of craving a storm
We're reborn through the depths of its conform
Therefore I must pursue the voyage of night
To bestow in that which is my light

<u>Nature: My Home</u>

Upon arrival, enticed by the evergreen's wit
Breeze of their desolate bark from its slit
And luring me in there lies I
Lost in its raveling, revery in traveling

The woodlands daunt me
As I shelter its leaves in my hands
And varnish the stones as if this were my land
Though however far I tread, home is upon me

For when I've attained my tracks
Evoked, I must go back
And the forlorn winds frolic through me
As they challenge my departure

Must I withstand the hues of its absence?
For when away, I *too* grieve their presence
And I perceive the warmth as a signal for assurance
That I won't abandon the roots of their endurance

May shade arise the light at the brink of dusk
For its greenery erodes when I am gone
And there lies I, winded by our seers
As the forest now depends on its own sweat and tears

Oh Mother Nature,
Though I know not why I deserve such pain
Could I best you merely this once?
For I cannot bear to yearn my refuge for months

Maybe

You were everything I didn't know I wanted
Perhaps it was the way you wielded my wings to safety
Or how you embraced me with your voice when out of arms reach
The moments in which you articulated your love,
Filling bullet holes of casualties that I've still yet to bury

Or maybe, just maybe, it's because it wasn't you
Your presence, not vacant, yet fragments of you were not
acquainted
Maybe I was so frightened to be left tangible again that I molded
myself in your image
Branding our minds together, thus excusing your behavior

Maybe. What a simple word, yet scavenges even the most elusive
parts of ourselves
Maybe it was all of those things, but I loved you nonetheless
So maybe there's hope for me after all
For if I can love someone that I mirrored,
Perhaps I can reflect on that so I may see myself clearer

The Sun

How must I describe the sun?
An endless source of light
Guiding all away from darkness
Yet not vengeful of its existence
A presence that brings warmth to all it encounters
And reason to anticipate tomorrow
The thing that gives life purpose
You, darling, are the sun

Old-Fashioned Love

I want that old-fashioned kind of love
The kind that doesn't make you question what you're in it for
Where we trade our love letters and depict the melodies of our
truths
The kind where we go on late car rides and stargaze our future
Traveling anywhere in the world so long as we're together
The kind of love where we dance without music or a crowd
Or running through a field in pursuit of a sunset
And settling down to savor when it rains
I want the kind of love that makes each day pass as though time
has not
Where abbreviations or one-night-stands are no longer an option
When love isn't changed or labeled as unfeasible
I want the kind of love that gives poetry more meaning
To the days in which affirmations were a frequent occurrence
As compared to now with hardly ever seeing it
I want the love that makes you garnish the minimal things in life
The kind that opens your eyes to all that lives on this wonderful
planet
I want the kind of love that has you being an entire world to
someone
And wanting to shield you from all that may bring you harm
Oh, how lovely that all sounds

Bird Calling's Ode

The sky timid in our pursuit,
As we migrate from its winds
Navigating our flock with the cloud's trail
And we find solace in the bearings of our birdsong
Like that of an untuned instrument regaining life

Though his forecast was evident,
As he could hardly keep up with the troupe
Merely pursuing the melodies of their tune
And upon autopilot's departure,
The blue's hues became clearer
Branching him adrift from his kindred

For the winds now blow crudely,
As he embraces his feathers, searching with ears
And for a fleeting moment, assurance is drizzled
Hearing the ode of his tribe
With the breeze swabbing his tears
As he's guided to his brethren's calling

Behold the beak of a lyrebird!
Whose tongue mirrors the rhymes of kin
Just as its beckon call within
And he bellows his siren,
Signaling the compass in wisps of
His song's breeze,
Being tethered from its guidance
Grieved by his own abiding silence

Nature and Its History Thank Him

The map was the man's compass,
As it navigates him through life's strife
Its dial, homing in sails over yonder,
Away from that of his own ship

When immersed in virgin lands,
Its untrodden ground mows a pathway,
Guiding the traveler with the whispering pines
Toward trees who yearn not to feel the soils' warmth

And the man's observant of its disconnect
As the grove drains its sun and water with no remorse,
Sprouting now as a thorn:
Lacking the knowledge of its maker's beauty

For he could depict deceit in their bark,
As not even their leaves were bestowed his sight
They merely gazed upon,
Yet not beholding that among them,
Splintering the glass of the voyager's map

Though despite the woodlands' ailment,
Its surrounding sites unleash their ancestors,
So they may whisper once more through the wind,
As they hone in his empathy of their fading realm,
And to rescue their souls from the depths of fate

Upon his arrival,
The mountains tip their hats and smile at him,
Its ancient ruins, too, euphoric by the man
And he embraced the warmth of their welcoming,
Absorbing the drought of their sorrows,
Carving the imagery of their bliss through his dial

Oh sweet Heaven, at home he was at last,
For nature, savoring his seedling with its roots,
And history, who salvages its pages with his muse,
Become his kindred — as however far they remain,
The winds will carry out their oath to one another

Though prior his ship setting sail,
They had graced him with their soot

To preserve him from the vengeful Red Sun,
Who's apathetic toward its trees
Though he is not of the same bark, no,
He is but an archaic oak, one with them,
And he has recuperated their lives, just as they did his
So now they grant him eternal life beside them,
As they're forever and always branded on his map

Tangible splatters of bullet holes caress the battlefield — its page,
Yielding each yesterday as an archivist's work; ancient, yearning not to tear blood
Planting purity amongst its patience, chiming to the writer's rhythm,
Examining the creation of its wielder, birthing me back to life
With mourning modern's bygone, my quill now one with its bird,
Refrained, in which our scribbler's nectar decays,
Incongruous with that of our current orbit
Therefore I savor morning's dew as it dawns,
Enticed by the olden orb's warmth,
Restoring the balance of earth's strife: Inscribing all within our minds

The Fundaments of a Paperclip

It begins with Lord Paperclip,
Oh, how divine he was;
A true prodigy at that
For he was our fruition to live
By being a decoy to the wind
And he forbade its chime from getting in
Though at what cost?

For he also combed the waves when they cried
As they clashed beside the shore,
Yearning for an ounce more,
Yet sponged by his magnet
And he retained them, all stagnant,
Hushing the tide with his hook
Though at what cost?

For he'd, too, bow in our presence,
Tangling us up in his temple,
Replenishing strength after each triumph
Against the taunting whispers
Branding we, his pages,
As we're sealed off for eternity
And now guarded by his chamber
With our only light: the he we choose to remember

For his catalog only grew with his empire
And he wielded us, our tree's silk,
As we're shielded from Mother Nature's will
For he was mightier than Mary's kin,
Imbued by the relics of our skin
And he was always quite famished,
Draining the ink from our unsoiled canvas,
Thus torn and bled, our damp got to the provisions

And the hunger bested him,
For the sea's whistle honed the Lord's sight,
Winding him, molding as the eye of the storm
That he had seamed his pages from
And he was struck by the rods of sin,

As he endured our suffrage from within
And Lord Paperclip had immersed all bent,
With his pages flooding the raft,
Along his dial's snapped sail; submerging in ink

It ends with Lord Paperclip,
Oh, how somber he was;
A true riddle at that
For he *was* our fruition to live
By being a conduit for the wind
And he forbade its chime from getting in
By heaving its tales within him
Though at what cost?
The veil of secrecy,
The loss of his mind and memories: his life

Synopsis:

Keep an eye on your paperclip,
Make sure it hasn't lost its pages;
Ensure it hasn't bent or snapped

What I Want

I want the road to be everlasting
To take me away from my companions
Who remain wilted from earth's sun
I want to stay in my mind's ladder
Each step a film strip,
Of mountaintops I become a scarf for
And keep warm every morn'
I want to drown out the tree's sap
To groom its leaves and harmonize with the breeze
I want to wipe its tears away
And watch as my presence makes it sway
I want to be enticed by the birds,
Who clock my days and tune me
Their ode; my anthem, navigating me by and through every night,
As though I'm one of their own
I want to be part of a flock
And I want to travel beyond the compass's view
To discover the silhouettes of this world
And recite the sightings of its maker's creation
I want to be the last human on earth
The one who preserves this very turf
Who salvages the beauty of the morning sky
Unlike my casualties, who abused its nature,
Thus deserving to die
I want the world to solely be seen through my eyes
I want the earth to be loved again
Is that all too much to ask?
For I just want to feel home at last

My Buoy

There's this saying about drowning
How we bask in the breaths of lost time,
The moments of survival, a muscle memory
Though who's there to save us, right?

For Cupid aimed at the wrong bay
And awake, I dare rest; though I must
As I await the trials of my final day

Though just as I'm overboard the plank
You've embodied me, my dear tank
Wrapping yourself around me,
Thus savored, both afloat and free

But how have you rescued and become my key?
For the days now mow the lawn
When our curtains prickle dawn

And I'm quite fond of you, my darling *Muse*
For you're the ink to my quill
The replenisher of my key's strains;
A typist's lovely companion, you are

See if I were to ever lose you,
I reckon the sea itself would part ways,
Guiding me back to that in which you are:

The ocean's conduit; the anchor that shalt never fall
Though if you must, thou won't for long
For I will inflate your lungs once more
And nurse you to life along the shore

And as my patience tests me, I will admire your essence
Just as I've done when acquainted with your presence;
For all it takes is your wave to engulf me in a whirlpool

Though when you're renewed, I shall sing you a remedy
One infused with my love, an absolute prodigy
Then we shall return to the boundless blue

Where I'll praise the auras of your hue

And from there I'll recite you this poem,
Requiting your embrace with the words of my grace;
Announcing it was you that kept me buoyant

Therefore I leave you with this:
Writing has always been the tree to my heart,
And you have been the most wonderful piece of art
That I've had the honor to write about and start

Fire's Extinguisher: Air's Fuel

Fire leaps from one gust to the next
And carried by Air, whose currents sketch into a smile
As he abides the embers of her blazing sun

Each spark, trotting the grounds of nature's confetti,
Etches their vapor to the soil of webbed roots;
Allowing the fallen to frolic in pursuit

Air dances with the dragon's inferno,
Her tongue lapping the skies to birth their offspring,
Crinkling the leaves to fate, hollowing out their debt;

Though behold! The wispy veil of mist and ash!
A token of their acquainted flare,
The artery to their cascading heart

And Fire latches onto her matchbox
As he's the quieter to her untamed fibers,
Quenching ignitions of the igneous hails

She then uses her exhaust to stifle the whispers
Ones that encase Air of taunts to let waste of the land;
And she revives his chivalrous charm and buoyancy

Though Fire also diffuses herself, tanning the sky;
So she may erupt and confine his foes with Holy Fire,
As she entwines with the transparency of his gusts

And Air absorbs the fumes of his match
As she's the replenisher to his turbulent breeze,
Sedating the bustled whispers of cloud's chime

He then uses himself as an aqueduct,
As he transports her oiled tears to sea,
Restoring her bonfire from catching ablaze

Though Air also whirls himself, the eye of a storm;
So he may wind her demons, with the aid of Holy Water,
As he interlocks the target of her ember gaze

Thus Fire and Air are not of Oil and Water
For they're imbued with the smoke of their seedling
As it roots them eternal, so long as they remain one

The Stagnant Steed

The tracks seemed everlasting,
Weaving itself around forbidden woodlands
And there lies I, the iron steed,
Who seeks to glide in the veiled blue
Trodding the soil of virgin skies and unspoiled lands;
Like that of a metal bird and its pilot

For the steed always appeared to be stagnant
Never pledging its track-bound melody,
Merely observing the barked graves
As they lured over her
And her wheels sparked the fumes of her exhaust
Against the railway veins of her longing;
Perhaps if she lied still for a moment longer,
A train would have rustled by
And strung her up like a railway pole;
Thus slow and steady does not conquer the race

Though a leafed titan emerged to relish the steed
They embraced her hatchet,
Supplementing the sobbing symphony of her leaks
To strengthen the roots of their bondage
And they tame their warmth in her brakes;
Branching the forlorn to the steed,
As they retain her grounded, and she keeps them earthbound

Yet still,
She finds herself not treading forward
For the reward appears unforeseen
The more she strides,
The more the current severs it from her stream,
Leaving her unable to reach it or scream;
And there lies the return of the stagnant steed,
Whose only hope is sought out by the reprieving wind
Along swerving stations due to the steeled tongue

The Shattered Mirror's Reflection

In the realm of shattered glass,
Behold the tale I've conjured!
Raptured by sin, the shards of my many reflections
Once divine, now obscured with visions of delusion,
Serving life through Kaleidoscope's Third Eye
With its fragments, who've yet to crack under the pressure of
blindness

Therefore I welcome you to trace the carvings of my maze,
Each vine stemming the roots of my tainted image
Uncover the truths of my shrine for me,
Open my veiled eyes, replicate light's purity in my demise;
Savor the source of my portal, and unite my prisms together
Grant me the sight to my looking glass: make me whole again

Oh please, toss me the rope from Heaven's Gate!

Beneath The Bark

In the garden of life,
A tree stands tall;
Offering shade to the forsaken,
Hailing his kindred with sap

The woodland bestows his place on the throne:
The Guardian of The Forest,
As he's set to rid the predator's shadows
Though underneath his barken coat,
His own infestation awaits

Cancer's cruel touch,
Etching its curse through the veins of the oak;
Spreading to the stumps of his bark
And soon stripped from his skull

Once radiant with hues of green,
Now obsolete, his last petal wilting;
Scars of nature's wrath imbued in him
As the exposed roots begin to weep,
Quenching the thirst of his disease once more

Yet within the trials of fate, there awaits anew
For in the face of his frailty
Sprouts the seed of the man he's longed to be
And there again, cupped by Mother Nature's hands;

The leaves that once weaved his deathbed
Now rest as his crown,
Nurturing its strained branches;
And his roots, woven with the guidance of their soil,
Embrace the earth tightly, whispering his thanks

Let the tree's tale be a lesson:
Through the ailment and realms of demise,
The Mighty Oak clamped his feathers like gems,
Taking a breath, his own at last; without its ribs in the way
And planted back into the ground
As the sapling he has always longed to be

To Whom It May Concern

To Whom It May Concern,

If you love me, just tell me
Don't slip it in my tea when I'm not looking,
Or needing me to erupt for you to want
To patch me up
Ah, right, it's always:
"Turn that frown upside down!"
"The world needs more of that precious smile!"
But what about me? The actual me;
Not just the vessel in which you wish to corrupt
You know,
The girl that's said to make something out of nothing,
Ushering curses of others to their wake
With the lullabies of her pen;
And Arthur's Blade that is her tongue,
Who makes remedies to keep the kindred young
Yet there she lies,
Gasping for the air that's been used on her spells,
And rotting away, not one by her side
To Whom It May Concern,
If you love me, just tell me
Don't embrace my petal's bed with flowers
And try replenishing me with your tears;
Offer me that sweet nectar of yours now
Tell me that you love me *now,*
Before the wind guides me North, not South

To Whom It May Concern,
It concerns me
Therefore I tell myself my own remedy:
I love you;
And now I have been reborn

The Inward Symphony of Solace

I guess it makes sense
When you're so used to their yelling
The moment you awake in bed,
You've begun to blare other voices in your head;
Odes that sweep you away for a while,
And express the words you feel denied to say

The melody that follows them,
Tangling your thoughts to strangle them;
An anthem to an unrequited sanity
And so you turn up its volume,
Hoping to run away from the dread;
Yeah, I guess it makes sense

Why you let your ears bleed inward
To stop hearing them scream

The Blessed Tears

Blessed are you for allowing your tears to flow,
For these are signs of mourning; thus you'll grow
Each drop of the broken sky, ripples waves of wisdom;
And the tide surfs back to sea, within your kingdom

The Dreams From Tempting Fate

Oh, how you were right;
It was a mistake tempting fate,
Trying to invent *future* when there's solely *present*
But I have dreams that aren't likely to flourish,
Which punish me to slumber in sheer daylight

As time sifts on, we become rivals;
Remaining still, yet forever in motion,
Making me a deer in headlights

For when the moon eclipses the sun,
My dreams are more vivid, alive;
And I only find myself truly living
In the moments where I'm directing ahead,
Where others nor I can see

I can't fathom how long its been;
Since I've lived beyond the walls of my mind,
And shied away from reality; all of mankind

Loose Ends That Should Stay Loose

I always find myself "tying loose ends,"
I guess my heart feels like it has to make amends
But somehow she always races for her life,
As in return I get strangled
And gashed with a knife

Should I use that blade to cut the same cord?
Or will I be more distressed if we're torn?
You've compelled me as your muse;
Though once I broke from your trance,
I'm more encased in your noose;

Yeah,
No more.

How (*I*) Poets (*Was*) Are Made

Sometimes poets are born,
Destined to be The Prophets of Word;
The Gatekeepers of earth's lore,
Able to recite the rumbles of each stone's core;
Through echoes of the wind
That only they can perceive,
You see the world for the beauty it truly is
Through the lens of their realm;
Not needing a moment to study it yourself

And other times,

Poets aren't born; they're created,
Forged into The Wells of Fate
And imbued with markings of their scars;
They mend their wounds through their tongues
By using their tales as the source of their words,
Getting you to view the world;
Not only for the beauty it truly is,
But for how what we endure
Guides us to our destined path

In my case,
It was being a poet

The Home That Wasn't Home

And as ember's embrace slithered into my home,
I find myself already afloat
As I'm kissed by the fiery touch of fate;
Each gasp draws breath of me to ash,
Spoiling me with the sun's wrath
For my tears fed the flames rather than put it out;
Perhaps it's because it was never home to begin with

Dawned by The Sun

When I awoke,
For once, the sun dawned on me,
As she gave me the brightest smile;
And in the warmth of her love's caress,
She whispers to me, saying,
"You're meant to be here, you belong,"
And to that I now rest each night
As I await the light of every mourn;
For she is right, I do belong:
Oh, how I belong indeed

Metamorphosis

Once a seed,
Dormant and underway;
Unaware of the beauty that awaits you,
Lies the birth of optimism's offspring,
Hatching on veins of your leafed home

From a caterpillar,
You began to emerge,
Cataloging your character,
A symphony of chapters
The ground soothed to your inched rhythm,
Oh, how comforting it felt
It was as if the soil wanted to part ways,
Engraving a path for you;
To seek shelter before Winter's arrival

And upon hibernation,
You kept safe within your book,
As you shielded yourself from Nature's force;
Welcoming the vibrance of each page,
Shedding the dull and sprouting
a new:
Seeing the world beyond its ordinary view;
It's beautiful how immersed you are in life,
From the leaf that sourced your lungs,
To now soaring above life's tongue:

You're a true monarch butterfly

My Tiger Stripes

Though torment has brought you upon me,
I am glad we exist in the same flesh
For however long I was taunted,
And as many ships have sunk boarding my sea,
You're the one who has always stuck by me
So I shall wear you proudly, as a token of my love
For each of your brush strokes,
Who burned my virgin skin,
Appear now as badges,
Honoring the strength of I
Who became nearly the fallen;
Though in doing so, I was gifted your grace
Thus the suffering was worth you obtaining your place

Grieving An Unburied Ghost

At least death is final,
Their six-feet below is proof they aren't coming back
You miss them, until your memories collide
Distorting their image,
No longer the person you're meant to grieve

But what about they whom I can't unsee?
The silhouette that lingers through facades,
Whispering to me in my dreams,
Reminding me of the touch I never felt
How do I forget a ghost who's not been buried?

Shackled Wings: A Plea For Freedom

Oh, my Lord,

Why have you cast me here?
From Eden to Ashes
Within the grounds of havoc,
Where misfortunes pile unto my wings,
Tethering me to life's conform;

In the soil of spoiled words,
Lullabies told through gritted teeth,
Songs only sung when first spoken;
This orchestra orbits disputes about harmony,
A realm that's plucked each vein to my harp;

Could what I have done been walloped by less?
For the world's not cured me of my sins
It has scorched my divine quill,
Making me a walking ape among them,
No longer an untainted soul;

Oh Father, hear me
I beg of thee, if not return me,
Then please, oh please: have mercy,
Put me out of my misery
Send me to Hell, the new Heaven's Gate!

For I can endure more heat from Satan's hand
Than by hollowness caused by Earth's sun;
But Earth was not always so cruel, was it?
No, its essence was snuffed out
By they whom we call the "Children of God"

Oh, my Lord, please just set me free

Torn Between Thorns

Oh, *Mother*,

How the pricks of your pines
Pierce my petaled tree
I seek your nectar, yet I am parched;
Though I'm felt by the clouds
Whose eyes speak my words;
Where I'm afloat, yet submerged in their warmth

The turf's greener than
The soot which rots beside me,
Nurturing my decayed hues:
They see through your thorns which encase me;
Though each blossom of mine you stroke
Wilts the reminisce of who I've become

And when you're not near,
It's as though your leeches have cleared,
Where my rose may now appear;
Though it'll never be enough,
For I'll always be struck by your needled teeth,
'Till it scythes the remains of my perched leaf

Oh, *Mother*,
Repent our turmoil within this shrine, won't you?

Know that people change and evolve overtime, through both age and experiences. When you choose to love someone, you're choosing, and **have** to, love a different version of them at some point — whether it's every day, every week, every month, or every year. If you only love one side of someone, for instance, a version from when you first met, you'll eventually love someone who won't exist anymore. Love isn't just to do with valuing what you see in yourself through another, or seeking what you need more of in your life. It's also about embracing all of who they *may* become, no matter what. It's about savoring the core morality of their heart and purity, taking those memorable moments together, and telling yourself that they will change; without losing your your warmth for them. That's the true commitment to love: Accepting that people change, and that it's okay.

People won't recall all of the things you did or said, but they will never forget the way you made them feel. I want to remind you that just because you don't feel like you make a difference in this world, doesn't make that contribute to the truth. You have the ability to make something out of nothing, and that is absolutely beautiful and rare. Take a moment to reflect on that. How your smile can end wars. The way your very existence can replenish someone's day, or even restore them back to life. Don't you **ever** discard the value your presence has on this world. For we need more of those precious wings that you carry. You do belong here, and I know you're here to make a difference within this planet. That you're here to make people see the beauty in themselves that they've been denied to believe. Just take a moment to really honor yourself. Admire the person you're becoming, and all of the lives that are indebted to you. All I ask of you is this: Don't question these words that you're reading, and for once, reciprocate that goodness you place on others unto yourself. You deserve to feel your air that inflates the lungs of others. So let it in; supply it for yourself.

I understand how hard it is to get lost in someone whom your mind has created fantasies of. How you're the director of a false narrative of someone you long for; though hear me when I say that it isn't real. Those moments aren't real, and I don't say that to wish you distress; I say this because I know what it can do to a person. That constant nagging of guilt, the deranged and suffocating feeling of only living when you're in your head. Now, there can be many reason for why you do this: You create life in the things and people that aren't likely to remain in your life long-term. You don't believe life can go your way and that you can't have it, all because it's what *you* want. You think life is against you. You savor the feelings you get from these daydreams because they're what you don't receive outside of them. The world behind your realms of conjured moments are filled with uncertainty, feelings of being unloved or unwanted; alone in a world of chaos. You have control when you're in your head. You aren't having to expect anything to go wrong because *you* have the wheel; you depict a life that you don't think you deserve yet crave for relentlessly. The truth of the matter is that you can't control the actions and feelings of others, let alone the future since it doesn't exist. There's only now, and believe me when I say that sourcing your feelings, and even who you are, into these daydreams are what's keeping you stuck. By placing your emotions into an idolized person or idea, you're allowing them to have control over **every** fragment of your life: If you don't hear from them, you don't think you *deserve* to start your day, but the second you do hear from them; you feel alive again. Learn to source your love and strength back into yourself, take back control over *your* life. Don't fixate on people that you've turned into saints.

Don't be hard on yourself for not accomplishing everything on your list today. Don't bash yourself for the things you *didn't* do without acknowledging what you *have* done. The things you choose to acknowledge, especially those that tie to the past, are all the things that merely contribute to knowing where you've *been*. They don't show where you're going or how you've grown, so take what you see as "failures" or an "inactive day" as progress, because it's showing your commitment and determination to getting where you want to be. Know that you're more than what you wish was different about yourself. For there are people who couldn't live without those exact things; and who are grateful to know you. That being said, only embark on change if the decision is solely inspired by **you**, and to better the relationship with **yourself**; not to mold into how others *want* for you to be.

We're such a traumatized generation that the protagonist is no longer who we aspire to be. We know the character well, yet hardly see them outside of fiction. And so it's now the villains we're drawn to, because the antagonists are just hero's with an origin story. Think about it, we've gone from looking at a villain and saying, "Wow, they're so messed up." to then, "Gosh, the world has really messed them up." And that's what we now relate to more, which is why we sympathize for them; as they're always misunderstood. I hope one day you empathize for yourself the way you do with them. Remember, it's not about what's been done, but rather what you do because of it.

The Penny That Became a Dime

And there they lay,
On the bustling streets of a rainy day;
Homeless within tunnels along the road,
One that the concrete split its sea for

A copper disc,
Whose infused with imprints
From Bill's knotted laces;
A coin not wanted, neither heads nor tails,
So away he soars, one less year engraved in him

For the penny has no place beside Bill,
As her status towers him tenfold
And so he aborts to abide beside the shore,
Letting the blows of his abuse wind him along

Though before he knows it,
He's webbed by a beaked collector;
One who caws at the sight of battered brass
She scoops him up with her pail
And tends to his wounds, untying the knot

As she lands on Nature's runway,
The ocean whirls and waves at him;
And the fish make peace with the sharks for a day
The sun stops reflecting, now beaming *just* on him

The penny gazed at its glazed aura,
Yet somehow not blinded; if anything, he saw clearer
For the cloud's halo smeared his coppered musk,
Retrieving his silver-lining: that in the right shade of light,
He was never a penny, he was solely a dime

I don't like to look at anger as a negative thing, though of course if you're putting others or yourself in danger then yes, it is. However, the emotion in itself is merely a reflection of what you consider to be mistreatment. Whether you're angry that someone wronged your friend, or even yourself, you're angry because you know they, or **you**, didn't deserve that. If not because of that, then you're angry at yourself for thinking you deserved that for so long, or that you couldn't convince your friend sooner. That anger is a mixture of sadness and feelings of stupidity for acknowledging that you didn't deserve it, but also feeling scared and alone because you entrusted that person with your love.

So there's a way to go about and look at anger. It isn't just a sole emotion; it's a collective of them that are used as a way to avoid the true emotion that you don't want to have felt on its own. Know that you don't have to look at anger as only lashing out and becoming physical, or punching a brick wall until your hand blends with it. Anger is about looking deeper into that emotion, understanding what exact moment ticked it off, and finding both the emotion you're actually feeling deep down, as well as what turned that previous emotion to portray as anger. It's all about identifying it. Don't look at anger as a "negative" emotion, because like I said, anger's a mask for how you're truly feeling about something.

Please don't live your life by societies expectations. Don't let yourself down because the world makes you feel behind. I can tell you right now that it won't matter how many diets you go on or how low that number is on the scale: If you don't have that admiration and love for yourself then that work will be absolutely pointless. Why? Well because it won't make you feel better in the slightest. Truth be told, I've been there; I've spent years believing that by living by modern-day's standards and stereotypes I would be happy and have the life I wanted. What did that do for me? It made me severely depressed, never knowing who I was, anxious to want to socialize and speak up about my problems, as well as hate the body I had regardless of if it was healthy or not. I was not being myself and *truly* living life. You may think you have to do all these things; be on a calorie deficit, workout vigorously, only post the highlights of your life, have a fear of being vulnerable or judged, figure out what you want to do with the rest of your life by a certain age, follow in your family's footsteps, yada-yada-yada, right? Listen to me when I say you do **not** need to live by this if it doesn't align with you. The main thing about life is finding yourself and being comfortable with the person you are because you're the **only** person you have to be with all day every day. So before you place your worth in the values of society, really ask yourself what *you* value. Once you establish those boundaries and love for yourself, everything else will no longer hold any weight or distress on your heart. Know that you're not expected to be what society wants you to be, and don't let their criteria stop you from achieving the life you want for yourself.

Typewritten Love

Don't type your love on modern keys,
Strain your hands on the rhythms of a typewriter
Spill your ink, flood the soul with your pages,
And pour them out as first drafts
Splatter hails of love with the dyes of your fingertips;
Make everything you say have meaning

Starlit Alignment

When I look at you,
I see a constellation in which we align in
Where each star is a reason to accompany the moon
Though despite all of them being different,
There's one thing which makes them harmonious to one another:
They all lead to you
Oh, my darling *Moon*, you're all I yearn for;
Whom I wish to eclipse from unlit heavens,
Blasting you away from voided skies

The Tale of Two Black Sheep

One morning I sat on a stone,
Though a mountain in my eyes,
And my father sat by me on a pebble,
Where I towered over him
See, he likes to open the owl hole of my tree,
Getting me to honor his love for this world
And I never understood it,
The way he briskly walked and made oceans follow him
Or how he'd make it rain to give
The roots a chance to live

Though there was something about that day;
For upon looking up at me, he says,
"We are our Shepard's black sheep
Now, don't wear that blandly;
For our coats are bestowed unto us,
Passed down through Messiah himself
His tears are our sweat,
And that in which we drink and bathe from;
Which then we cycle out of us,
Flooding it back into the ground, our ocean bed:

Thus is the blood of rarity, our purity
Which is why the Devil will send his bishops for our heads"
I honestly wish I'd of known what he'd meant,
For with the flick of my skipping stone,
The waves had hit us,
And the tide took him away;
Never seeing him again
And now I bask on this mountain,
Nearly three years and counting;
Awaiting to follow our destined path,
To walk in his footsteps

Seeing You Bare

Is it wrong of me to want to see you naked?
Now I don't mean stripped of your fabrics
I mean shed from the cracks that you wish to hide,
The ones that have you feeling confined;
Love, please let me in to open the drapes,
Allow my light to cast over you;
For if you could only see yourself through my lens,
You'd gain sight on why I'm not the rest
You're not a thing that I want to displease;
But a heart that deserves being desired
And that, my dear, is why I wish to see you bare;
For I want you free of our world's curse,
I want to see *you*

The Stenographer

She savors words of the unspoken,
Or what she claims to be said of her kindness;
Though they rarely are
And when she picks up her pen to clock-in,
She's met with the dials of dread
For she's of vials of acquainted secrets,
Organized in order of her inked bed;
And yet hers await art's embrace,
A canvas seeking the strokes of her own imagery
Why must she conjure the lives of others
When the mirror's met with her client's pages?
When will she put down her pen to clock-out?

Farewell to Unclaimed Love

How does it feel, hmm?
To lose the person who'd sail
Seas of untamed waters for you
Who lied about synchronizing with your sleep,
In case you sought a pillow to entrap and keep you safe;
To lose all of the jokes that I'd sing for you,
Or the poems of you I'd recite at night
How about the woman who saw you the most?
Who fiddled your strings and inspired you to be tuned
What about the girl who made the boy feel seen?
Or the lady's love that sparked such safety in you?
She who hung her words on dangling branches
Instead of clinging them for herself
Yeah, how does it feel?
To lose the one person who has always been there;
Never once asking for as much in return
You know, you once asked me who I thought I was,
And to that I say this:
I am the only one who will ever love you this way,
Thus I wish you the best with whomever's next

The Light in Forbidden Love

There's something so beautiful about it:
A love you cannot have
It involves with wines of sanity
For however much you pour into someone,
You'll always get lost in their weeds,
Drafted in their drained yet everlasting river;
Leaving you submerged in the nothing of it all
And as the wind whispers that in which
You can no longer hear,
You refuse it once more,
And listen to clashes of waves along the shore;
Instilling it'll work out somehow,
Making you feel helpless,
Not wanting a way out
It's honestly the worst type of love
For it is neither of your faults,
Yet you grieve them as though you aren't one without the other
Though I find it wonderful all the same,
How just within, you say it's not your sin to bear
And even if you can't see it yet;
You'll feel it until it crashes in waves,
Like the clashes you chose over your truth
It's lovely how they correlate, wouldn't you say?

The Bird in The Cage

I'm loved by you from afar,
Seen as a souvenir - kept hidden behind bars
When I hear my brethren at sunrise,
I wish to squeeze through this cellar;
And though I can't fly since
You've stolen my wings,
It would all be worth it;
To have the last thing on my way down
Be the sounds of those who
Display their praise for me

This is your reminder that you aren't going to be liked by everyone. There will always be at least one person who won't like you for the sake of it, and that's okay! Know that it's okay to disappoint people, it's okay to not gain their approval. There's always a reason we cross paths with those in our lives, both who are still with us and who are not. You either meet them to change your perspective and learn about yourself and what you seek in others, or you're the one who helps them see that in themselves. Don't live your life trying to receive acceptance from everyone else, you'll just be displeasing yourself with a goal that isn't achievable. Instead, seek validation within yourself.

There's a difference between someone who makes time for you versus someone who only speaks to you when they respond. You know, the kind who says they'd choose you, yet forget what's spilled from their tongue moments later. Listen, my dear, settle for someone who doesn't make you question what you both are. Show all the parts of you to those who have earned the right to. For you're not someone who you come by every day, thus people have to deserve to know you. Choose people who don't make you seek for a sign that all's fine; because you asking for one provides an answer in itself.

The Debt We Owe

How many breaths will you take by the end of this poem?

I love the idea of people,
Just not *these* people;
The kind who wipe your tears
Into the drains they came from,
Who prefer to hear you
When it's not *your* name in your mouth

And perhaps that's why I'm sunken,
For I seek to rid the earth of its toxic waste;
Of unappreciative mouths who
Murder those that gift us our very breaths
From reading this page aloud,
You'll have lived about five gusts longer

Let us be they who give life meaning,
The ones that place buckets out for the rain
And supply back to the trees,
Ounces more of what they've just received
We owe it to the world for creating its core;
Let us refund to those who grant us life

I hope you feel more grateful to breathe and be alive

Anchored Devotion

So long as I'm cast as your anchor,
You will have someone to carry you
From the depths you sink
And as you zip-line through my chain,
I shall take your place at the bottom of the ocean;
So you don't get caught on Satan's hook

Mapping My Inner Landscape

I am of shattered sand,
Not ever made into glass
I am of a blackened home,
Its ruins plastering my heart
I am of hurricanes with stillness,
Stuck in disasters of a place I long to leave
I am of ragged nests not mounted on branches,
Cracked open; not waiting 'till I've hatched

Though I am also of wind for fallen leaves,
Escorting them to their trees,
Stemmed from our bonded belittlement
I am of streams of pure screams,
My delicacy frothed up on its shore;
With waves brushing up to a smile
I am of passed down narrators,
As I sift through the tales of my quill
I am of winded lungs
Through the storytelling of puns

I am of sheltered yet broken bones,
With splintered muscles within
I am of pebbles and stones,
Both an outcast yet divine
Though through all this I shall survive,
For this skeleton will restore itself
Into the image I've longed to be
Thus I am also of growth:
I am enough

The Vintage Cafe

I step down the railway
To a gateway beyond;
The Castaways Cafe
A portal of realms to get away
Its darken lights brighten the
Lens of my Third Eye,
As I feel Hell's grip loosen my mind
And now I sit,
Birthing all shades of brews;
Poems of my different hues
In a scenery I shall call my new home

Although I can't always be there with you, I will **always** be there *for* you. You should never feel that you will be put in a position where you will lose me. For if I were to even die, I'd be there to caress you through each day. I would blend with your shadow, forecasting that you aren't alone. And when night prickles, I shall morph as the bulb of your lamp; to be kept lit until I get the luxury to watch you sleep, and repeat it all over again when you awake. In other words, you needn't worry, my dear: I will always remain here, for death does *not* do us part.

Ask yourself this: Why is it that I seek the approval of those who don't know me? How come I care about the opinions of people that **I** don't know? When will I stop fearing judgment from voices whose advice I wouldn't take?

My Invaluable Artifact

If I were given an Orb of Dawn
For each time I thought of you,
The world would be rid of Ebony's reign
And if I gained a penny
For each day I have loved you,
Then I'm of both riches in life
One fulfilled with yachts and bills
And the other;
Obtaining the utmost value there is,
Which is you
For when we speak,
I cut the outlet from our clock,
To ensure time is not of the essence
Yet still,
In the moments of each goodbye for the night,
I hear my drum more than my thoughts;
As if the hourglass sifts through our paused time,
Never making it enough:
Our roots of woven forests are still yet brisk
And like the wind, you carry my breath away
With the nestling of your oral pen,
Making the pages of my book leap
Yet all in the same, I thank you
For beating my breathless heart

Cherish Your Seeds

I am so madly in love with you,
You hopeless romantic
Oh, my heroic companion,
I am fond of the ways in which we're alike
How you scoop the puddles of muddy eyes
And cup the faces of inner hearts;
The way you sing to the chirps of mayhem
So your voice may travel among the vacant
I adore how your words smile for you,
And how your lips pour into my grazing grounds
It is a miracle I have found you
For you are of clouds, both whom come and go
Thus I will cherish you in this moment,
And the ones after this very day
I will accept when you must let me go,
For you'll eventually run out of seeds to plant;
And must carry on to where the wind takes you
Though if you could do **one** thing for me when it's time,
Don't *just* bury your seeds in the next person's soil
Also enroot them in yourself, my love;
Use those harnessed tears you've collected
To quench your thirst and watch yourself grow
Don't sprinkle such safety in those you meet
Only to migrate to seasons that have yet begun;
Savor that for yourself as well,
Allow yourself what you give to everyone else
Don't distribute yourself poorly,
Realize the impact your presence has
Not just its value when you go,
But when you embrace people the most;
That is all I will ever ask of you

The Burden You Need Not Bear

I hope you know that
You do not have to be sturdy here
Lay your veil of sadness unto me,
Allow me the gift to hold you in ways
In which you weren't granted before
For you are not a sunken ship
Whose meant to be buried among treasure
You are a buoyant sailboat,
One that will tame seas to wave at turbulence,
And restore them to calming waters;
You are valued more than what you provide,
Let me show you

You *Do* Believe in Love

You say you don't believe in love anymore,
Yet the glimmer in your eyes
When around nature tells me a different lie
Or how you look down on the starry night,
Both canvas and a true hued sky
With tears of comets welting your eyes
You say you don't believe in love anymore,
Yet I believe you're wrong
For I watch you comb the petals of flowers,
Never daring to pluck them from their homes
I watch you immerse in novels of life,
Forgetting time in the words of possible worlds
I watch you dance in the bustling rain,
And rewarded the aroma it leaves
I watch you dial the number to your heart,
In those who are blocked from receiving it
I watch you paint pages without color,
Creating forms of art that can only be imagined
And I watch you hug trees as if today is their last,
Swearing their branches caressed you back
So you see, you do believe in love,
You just don't believe others do
Which is why your love is placed in things
That aren't of the people;
And that's okay

Quit tallying each person that leaves your life and making it the reason you don't matter. You absolutely do, you've just met people who are too blind of their own problems to see your value and how lovely it is to have you in their lives. Anyone should feel lucky to know you, so be grateful that you get to be with yourself more than anyone else.

Tumbleweed tumbles so it can spread its offspring and give them a better chance at surviving. They branch from their homes and shower the grounds with their essence. I hope you can be like a tumbleweed: Someone that can take the environment that has caused them much torment, and be able to detach from it and its dead-rooted opinions. I hope you can shape yourself and love what you see so much that you wish to inspire others to feel the same. I hope you learn that you're enough and will plant life in places that are believed to be rotten.

Hear me when I say that unless you are being told directly, the inner monologue of judgement that you have are your own thoughts about yourself. You have been warped to believe that because you do not look like those who are labeled as the standard, you are lesser, and that people are actively seeing that in you. Allow me to remind you that you are not your thoughts. You are more than what you have been blinded to see. Do not let your thoughts perceive you and become your critic. I can assure you that the things you overthink about, whether it's to do with your choice in clothing or a conversation that's been had, all of the thoughts racing through your mind are reflections on your self image, not how people think of you.

To My Soulmate

Hello, you
We haven't actually met yet,
But I keep having dreams of you
I envision a world in which we
Kayak the streams of countries,
Where we scrapbook our travels
And bring value to living
I think about waking up to the sight of you,
Not having to meet Death to see Heaven up close
I think about how quick our days would feel,
From savoring each moment I'll be with you
How lone walks along the beach turn into
Towering waves with you as my surfboard
I think about the poems I'll write for you,
And watch as you melt between my arms with each one
I know we haven't actually met yet,
But I'm looking forward to the day we do
Though until then,
I shall be my own soulmate
So in that case,
Hello, *me*

My Inner Child

I was never hungry for food,
Though I was starved of bedtime stories
Of hugs I wouldn't be grateful for,
Though I now deprive for never having
I was drained of my youth,
Forged into the Elder's dictionary;
Never fitting with those my age
She was taken from us before her time,
And I have longed her return ever since
I hope she finds her way back home

Whispers Under The Moon

I once called the man I secretly loved
And told him to go outside so he could
Look up at the moon for me
When he stood under the tainted sky,
I told him,
"I'm looking at the same moon right now"
He took a moment, then replied,
"I know, I can see your eyes through the moon's stream"
And I pictured his beaming face on that rock,
Which helped give my reply
"I see you too, though not just now;
I see you in the voids of shut eyelids
Thus I can see you all day and night,
A gift I never wish to lose"
Which left him utterly speechless

When someone gives you signs to let them go, you do so. Not because you don't love them, but because you love yourself more. Not because they're too busy, but because they're too busy to prioritize you. Not because you're not good enough, but because you're slowly losing yourself in trying to save a relationship with someone who isn't reciprocating what you give. Not because you're asking for too much, but because they don't care what your asking for and how much it means to you. Not because there aren't enough hours in the day, but because they choose to spend those free hours without you. Not because you're "too sensitive," but because you've had enough of only hearing from them when it's convenient. Not because they can't be comedic and caring towards you, but because they mainly are when you supply it first. Not because you can't share the parts of you that no one knows, but because they don't honor or care how rare it is to hear those things about you. Not because they're incapable of showing affection, but because they don't value you enough to want to express it. Not because they need time to find themselves, but because they don't acknowledge how much you got them through their hardships, and how they'll let you go once they find whatever it is they're trying to find. This is your sign to leave them: If you've read all of this and connected dots. If you've been asking for a sign, that on its own is one. If you've been the only one wondering when they'll get back to you, when they'll call you, ask to hangout. If you question why they haven't shown up for you as much and try to justify it with the minimal good that they've done. Let them go. It's time to focus on yourself. They will feel the loss once you're gone, and if they don't, that is a lesson they will feel the pain from with the next person they meet.

The Corpse of Love

He told me goodnight for the last time,
And neither of us knew it would be so
For when I walked the staircase home
I saw a corpse with a soul locked inside
He shouted from within,
Banging on his eyelids to open,
Quivering his mouth to speak;
But he couldn't
And that was when I truly loved poetry
When I could ease one's pain
Through the songs of my words
For I sat and sung what I had created for him
And in that very moment,
I knew he was alive,
Yet only held by a thread
For he shed tears that spoke back to me,
Reminding me how loved I am,
Hugging me through his teeth
And when he took his last breath,
Our tears collided into one,
As they trickled down the same cheek
His skin as rotten as my molded heart,
His touch as cold as my numbed gaze
When I felt his heart stopped,
Mine skipped to try and save him
And when his Third Eye shut,
I could no longer see what recited color
When he died,
The last thread of my youth went with him;
I've been trapped in a child's body ever since

Unexpected Solace

Two caterpillars cocooned me today
Not because they wanted to,
But they felt like they had to
For I was a sun-kissed woman on her tanning bed,
Half deprived of thoughts and nearly passed out
I haven't been embraced in a long time,
And I couldn't hold my tears back any longer;
It felt good to be wrapped by arms
That weren't my own for a change

What's Your Haven?

I was once asked what my favorite place was,
And even still I can't answer
For my home is not of confined walls,
They close in on me;
As each coat of paint is splattered on them,
Layering the seas of uncharted anchors
No, see, my place is within people,
They whom make Time of Day's
Metronome tick faster
For there are 365 days in a year,
Yet I'm still stuck on day 1
I guess I've not found my people thus far,
Therefore I've not sited my haven
Though even then,
I await the day someone sparks
From my fumes of flourishing flames
For as long as I take breath,
I will keep the cold from seeping in
For as long as I'm alive,
They won't go a day without feeling loved
I suppose that's my answer

Awakening in Another's Gaze

She sat in the rest chair of a great oak
And read a poem that made him love her
Does she know I used to write him
Lullabies to put him to sleep?
For my words allowed him to rest,
As hers kept him up at night
Does he see me through her,
Or is he kept awake from how
Alive he is with her?
At least more than he ever was with me

~ *Replaced*

Chiaroscuro of the Self

I look at myself and see a sunset
Each colorful hue,
So tinted and true,
Washing the sky to farewell our dear sun
But it's fiery musk also erupts,
Clouding the skies, a smokey view;
The ash of my destruction
It's hard to be something so beautiful,
Yet wielding the power to
Pluck that very existence

Lost and Found

I misplace my bag of frozen peas,
Now a top hat to my fridge,
Thinking it was stored inside its head
I misplace my taste,
Savoring soured spit from rotten fruit;
Wishing to stir them into honeysuckle
I misplace my mom's credit card
That held my hand prior
And now I look seeing double,
With no signs of what I must find
I misplace my sight,
The lost cause within others;
Where I seek to bring those parts of them to life
I misplaced my priorities

Tangled in Favors

Why are you God's favorite
When I was your savior?
I held your hope in my hands,
My fingertips blue from the
Water you were denied to drink
And whilst you mummified away,
Your secrets wrapped me alive
Where I now walk coffined,
Unable to hone a word
Why are you God's favorite
When your pain casts through me?

Adrift in Solitude

When I say I am lonely,
I do not mean I need company
I am lonely in which
No amount of people can fix
For what I seek in the world,
The earth orbits away from
And the wings I try to grab,
Drag me down to this place;
Where we're meant to call home,
Where *I'm* meant to call home
When I say I am lonely,
I mean I exist in stilled time
With all else in motion
For the frailty of man toughens by life
And there is I,
Whom rots from its very sun
Thus I can never belong under the stars
I am forever out of place;
Destined alone for eternity

Fireside Reflections

When does it get quiet?
To extinguish my hopes for a s'more fire,
Sat beside shared logs;
Toasting to our branched faith,
My kindred critters of the forest
Yet here I am,
The gas of flames etching my path
As I'm left grilled by its grip
Alone on the logs' corpse,
Drenched in the fog of my blazing thoughts
And then it sparked on me:
What if finding solace in being stranded
Means to stop feeling anything at all?

The Dark Year

I stood before my disciples
Holding one of our own in my hand,
And I ate the remains of my sins that day,
Washing it down, my saliva of guilt,
That has since leeched onto my throat;
And forbids me to take true breath
For it was I who had slaughtered my people,
As survival was nothing to them
If it meant feasting on our brethren
And so I locked their souls behind bars too,
Hoping to hone my remaining warriors
Though in turn the graved are inside of me,
Tearing through my cement walls;
Its bricks beginning to weep
Though I had not wished this upon us
For it is her to blame, not I
She was the broker to our greatest demise,
The starter to the fighting pit
With its ground plastered in our crimson pulse
And its fenced border,
Who shields us from the evil in us all
Thus there they await,
The casualties we consume
In order to carry our name out,
Out into the vacant void of our lives
But hear me,
Oh I beg of thee, hear me,
That wasn't a law I had bound alone
For my hand was forged by a woman,
One who had cursed my armor,
Branding it the ink of our enemies;
And bestowing me the mark of shame
For crimes committed through me

Turning Stone: Medusa's Curse Reversed

I turn all who look at me to solid rock,
Their gaze a looped frame
They're never returned whole from that day,
With cracks awaiting to split them in half
Yet when I look at you,
The dust under the riverbed whirled clear;
Its rippled glass now a path
For you saw beyond the vines of my veil,
You glimpsed through my venomous eyes
And haven't stopped since
Thus I thank you, darling,
For getting me to look at myself
Without the fear of growing still
And in turn, curing my curse:
Turning those who look *at* me
Rather than *through* me
To stone
Thank you,
For showing me who I've been all along,
Away from who I'm conjured to be

Don't be manipulated into silence
By those who choose not to care
About how their actions make you feel.

Dear *You*,

You have been shunned of love for ions,
Forced to believe you forged your own fate
And so I picked up my quill and wrote you a letter
One that stated,
"In case you have not been told such:
Although there are many things to fond over,
And while there are many to cherish,
You are my favorite one;
And I smile as you exist alongside me
My only hope is you have now smiled too"

May we cross paths once more, dear friend
For I am only *truly* living
When graced with your presence

Love,
Cas

~ *My letter to you*

Know this, whatever it took to keep you here today, **you** did it. **You** obtained the triumph to breathe and thank the trees an extra day. Let that sink in, **You** survived yourself. **You** proved life wrong. Hear me when I say you're stronger than you know. All I hope is that you begin to give credit where it's due, because you have been victorious in many wars with the help of no one but yourself

Loving you made me
Lose a part of myself that
I never even got to understand

I hope you know that you always belong. Nothing you do or say can change that. You are here to leave an impact on this world and the people within it. Don't be afraid to be a leader, to show others how they can head down a path that has an end and forge their own trail from there. Don't be afraid to exist as you are, for there is absolutely nothing wrong with you.

Sometimes things happen to us unexpectedly, and our initial thought is to victimize ourselves. But what if we're meant to undergo all that we endure to become the best version of ourselves? What if each lesson teaches us more about ourselves than we realize? Maybe things happen *for* us rather than *to* us.

I'm grateful that I get to know you. To come across someone as graceful as you is irrefutably rare, thus I cherish each moment I get to spend with you. Thank you for still being here despite given all the reasons not to be. Thank you for waiting it out with me. For I'd rather be there to hear you tell your story once more than have to recite it for you. I promise you life will get better, you will go on. And I'm proud to be by your side at all times, especially now, fighting this war of yours to be okay with existing. You will feel alive again, you have my word.

One day it'll hit you, how you've spent majority of your life closed off from the world. How you thought it would protect you by doing such, how better you would feel by being treated as you've been taught you deserved to be. That you spent so much of your time and energy on those who refused to see you as anything but someone to use. I hope when this day comes, the day your eyes fully open to what you didn't deserve, I hope you won't be so hard on yourself. I hope you acknowledge that you did what you thought was best for you at the time for your protection. It's not your fault for being proven that you only mattered when you were supplying for others what wasn't given to you in return. Don't blame yourself for growing up in an environment that denied you from feeling truly loved. Instead, applaud yourself for getting to the realization that you didn't deserve to go through all of what you have. For you deserve to feel alive and a part of this world, you deserve to feel as though you belong here. I hope that day will be a celebration for you, and not just a funeral to the version of you who believed you didn't deserve to be treated fairly for the longest time. If anything, I hope today is *that* day for you.

Lost in Her Canvas

As her brush swipes its final sweat onto the canvas,
She rinses her mind beside her brush
And when she returns to her easel,
A man,
One she had recognized,
Is stood in her place
Etching his own landscape
The longer she eyed him,
The more distorted he became
And so the woman approaches the man,
Destined to know his true face
Though as she got nearer,
His gradient musk had become prominent;
As he began to fade out with his merged tones
With her last swooping step to look at him,
His eyes had fused with hers
And as she turned to the painting once more,
She was met with hers,
Where the man was stamped along a shore,
Created by her very hand
It had remained all along,
The woman couldn't fathom it
I have seen a man with all, yet no color;
Who's not of sand nor water,
One I have made from scratch
How has my character stood before me?
What stopped me from seeing my sculpture?
More importantly,
How had my work collided with his?
She rubbed both of her light bulbs
To ensure they were tuned
As she returned to where
She had placed down her brush,
The woman stared at the inked potion before her;
Its splatter of color mixed to one
Had begun to daunt her
And as she studied it,
With squinting eyes about to sizzle,
She had discovered its secrecy:

For she had strained her eyes with dyed vision,
Getting lost in the strokes of her own realm;
Warping her gaze for a time
Just as the brush had done
With its final note

If you have to beg for the simplest of things, perhaps it is not you who is asking for you too much. Your environment has simply refused to supply what you need. That doesn't make you a burden, it just means you're looking to grow in the wrong soil.

The only people who are allowed to have conflict with you are those who have been in your life for more than one sitting. If you're being criticized by someone who has only spoken to you once, they don't know you well enough to have a reason to be right.

The part about losing you that tore through me
Was the realization that there will come a day
Where I will have remembered you
Longer than I have known you
And I'm not sure if I will ever be ready for that

People are allowed to feel hurt by something you have done, even if you didn't mean for it to. They are allowed to validate their current state with your words or actions towards them. That doesn't mean you should downplay their emotions by trying to prove them wrong. That doesn't mean you need to get verbally vulgar in hopes to defend yourself, or needing to convince them that there is a misunderstanding to why they are hurt. That doesn't mean you should call them too sensitive or dismiss how they are feeling just because it doesn't make sense to you. None of that is helpful for them or yourself. As individuals, we are given aspects of our lives that are both in and out of our control. How we react to a situation is a **choice** or a trauma response; by thinking that reciprocating or shutting down what's presented in front of you will protect you given past experiences. *They* get to decide how something makes *them* feel, as do you in return. It doesn't matter if they are "wrong," that is how they feel by whatever it is you have said or done. Feelings are feelings. There is nothing untrue about them, people feel how they feel by the way they perceive situations. If someone says you have hurt their feelings, don't ignore it. Don't belittle them, don't mock or laugh at them. Instead, if you truly care about them, talk to them. Uncover what exactly upset them. At the end of the day, it's about taking accountability for the way **your** actions have effected someone in a way that was not intended for them to. It's about looking at it from **their** perspective and expressing empathy for how your behavior came across as how they described it. It's okay that you didn't mean to hurt them. As long as you acknowledge *why* and *how* it did regardless, *that* on its own goes a long way, more than you may think.

Unveiling The Unseen

It's hard to feel understood,
Being at war with scars
That you and I can't see

It honestly drives me crazy,
Thinking all of the time
Having to second guess each and
Every thought that comes to mind

And I fear when it's quiet too
Ironic how I push away
The thing I want most
But my mind races louder than
Its thoughts when there's silence

Will I ever find peace
Apart from when I'm asleep?
Am I as forgettable as the silence
Makes me seem?
How do I heal from pain that
Hasn't physically hurt me?

I question the origin of my suffering
For I have no memory of its soil
Nor its roots to my recoil
And I suppose that's just it:
When it comes to inner wounds,
It's not always about what happened
Sometimes, it's about what *didn't*

A Reminder From Your Inner Self

Allow me to remind you that
How you've been shown love is not
Consent to your acceptance of it
We expect the love we think we deserve,
And hear me when I say that
You are not fit to live in a
House with no chimneys
You are not deemed unreachable,
And you are definitely not worth
Being a stranger to anyone;
Let alone yourself
Allow me to remind you that
You are capable of being loved
No matter how many times
You've been instilled otherwise

Nurturing Your Essence

I hope you find what you're looking for
I hope you wake up tomorrow and
Feel blessed by being the first thing you see
I hope you speak up for yourself more
I hope you embrace your words tightly
I hope you learn to make choices for
you and **solely** you
I hope you learn to be okay in your own skin
I hope you don't define your worth by
The expectations of others
I hope you allow yourself to be seen,
To feel loved in the ways you make others seem
God, I hope you know you're someone worth knowing
And I hope the world won't make you disappear one day,
I hope you're the one who can make it bright again
I hope you know you matter

Sometimes we need to be immersed
In the darkness in order to realize
What our interpretation of the light is

Maybe loving yourself again starts with
Relearning the things you once adored
And valued in your younger years
In order to know when and what
Snuffed them out of you, and why.

Nothing that's worth doing or having is ever going to easily be feasible. It takes time and effort, and that's okay. You have to get used to the feeling you get *after* doing something rather than how you feel *before* or *during* it.

The Embrace of a Strangled Heart

I am of double knotted people
Those who cling to others for
Warmth they never wore
They yearn, yet fear, of being held in return;
In case it suffocates them till they're bare
They're artists, visioners
Who shape their laces into railways,
Getting lost in the crevice at each stop
Until it all ties into its very first knot,
Tightening around the whistles
Of their engine
And making it even harder to breathe
The more trips they take,
The worse it gets to wake
As each lap around the track
Loops its bunny ears an extra mile
Oh, the grip it has on them,
Forming rings of fire on their arms
With cherry flavored charms,
Carving its oath into their washed out skin;
Digging the lightning out of their soiled clarity
And though it's torn them beyond repair,
It's the only thing that's ever latched on
As a plea to remain by *their* side
It's the only contact they'll ever accept:
The inclusion of a noose

Your fear of being alone is actually just dreading to have a relationship with yourself based on how people treated an authentic version of you that was once shown to them. It's time to break that comfortability you have in the discomfort of your scathed image; so you may learn to fear living *without* you for a change.

Her Favorite Subject

I lend my pen to him,
So he may sketch himself in my notepad
Though soon his eyes will come to life
For he is of a blank sea
Awaiting to be splattered by a writer's print
If only the world could be of such
Able to see the good in the man
Through the tides of his life,
Not washing her portrait of him away
For she is of a poet`
With he as her muse

To My Future Child

Oh, my sweet child,
Although you cannot see much now,
And though you know not of your relevance to me,
I oath you a love far deeper than the oceans
For not even *she* could swallow you whole
And you will reach farther than the stars,
Outshining our moon, shaming its skies;
Even the North Star would stop to look at you
For gazing at your eyes would
Be to look at the world all at once
Therefore, I promise to shield you from fields of strife,
So the world may not take you from me
I will speak of you to the flowers,
Who'd wilt if obtained the droplets to envy
And you shall never fall by my hand,
Nor be scathed by my drawing breath
For I will not become the eyes
I had first dawned upon,
She who sewed my petals shut
I do not wish to show you the world, my dear,
I want it created by your sketch
May you not be taunted by false adversaries,
May you find comfort in your mind,
In me, in the divine that can be life
And should you choose to sprout your wings and fly
I shall be there,
To hold you tight one last time
Before I let you go and await for you home
So go,
Venture and see what's beyond our view
And when you return to me,
I shall grasp you, with a woven embrace,
And water my garden — which will last for days
As when you are with me,
It's as though life is given a meaning
Oh, my sweet child,
Know that you will never lose
Your place by my side,
Never in a thousand years

For how ever far away you are
And as many years to come,
You will always have the key to my heart,
Though I shall always leave its door unlocked

I'm glad that you're here today. I'm glad that you were here yesterday and the days before that. It's not always easy to be positive everyday, so don't spend more energy trying to. It's okay not to be okay, and it's especially okay to need a break from time to time. With this modern age, we're quite susceptible to falling into a void of not feeling as though we belong, but hear me when I say not to underestimate the consequences that your absence would leave. I want to remind you that you have something to offer to the world, and you spark the lives of others without realizing it. Know that you're wanted here, and if not felt by those physically around you, then by me — by the people also reading this page, by those who you'll soon meet that'll prove to you that you aren't incapable of being loved. I want you to know that you should give yourself more credit. You know, maybe you did get help from someone, but it was **you** that enforced that change, and that's not easy to obtain motivation to start, let alone accomplish it. So wake up every morning and be proud of yourself for living, because I'm proud of you! I want you to know that you're very much loved and that you aren't alone. You aren't a burden or a waste of space and energy: You're someone who's worth all the time in the world, and someone who I think is worth knowing.

I hope you know that it's okay to go at your own pace. Not everything has to be achieved by a certain point in time, especially when it comes to your personal growth. It's okay to go backwards, that doesn't mean you have had a setback. It means you need to be shown what lesson you've yet to learn. You aren't falling behind, don't worry. You're exactly where you need to be. Don't rush the journey of healing, for *that* is where you actually learn.

The journey to finding yourself when you haven't known who are for so long will not be easy. Perhaps that's why most choose not to. They give up, afraid to see beyond the consciousness that is their minds. I don't say this to derail you, but because someone needs to care enough to be honest with you. It's going to hurt. You're going to uncover things that you subconsciously intended to keep buried. You're going to be physically exhausted by all of the thinking and scavenging. Yeah, it's not going to be pretty, but you know what else you earn from this? You get to learn more about yourself, **you**; someone who deserves to feel comfortable in their own skin. You'll get to feel at home within yourself. You'll get to learn what ignites you, what weighs you down, and the types of people you wish to have around. It is through the suffrage of inner blindness that you open your eyes to the path ahead. So although you're not given much of a reason to, trust the turmoil that is carried inside of you, for it'll be your guidance to the light; the map to finding out who you are.

You do not owe your family anything when they've stripped away your perception of life. You do not have to invalidate your feelings because of how they claim you make them feel in return. Even though you may hold this weight of guilt with thinking you're at fault, you aren't the one who has a responsibility to nurture you; that's *theirs*. You do not need to feel sorry for withdrawing your love for them. All it has done is give them another chance to make you think love is not feasible to you. And oh, how false they are, I promise you. I know how the absence of a familial bond can mold your mentality. How you think you can't be loved for who you truly are, so you push away from people the moment they show you any light of day. I know. Hear me when I say you are **NOT** incapable of mattering just because the ones who were meant to chose not to. Their mistreatment of you doesn't make you worth any less, it doesn't make you a burden on anyone's shoulders. Just because you were denied love from others, it does not instill that you aren't deserving of receiving it. And just because you've been abused to assume that your voice isn't heard does not give you permission to silence yourself. What you have to say is important, and the right people will cherish your words to their graves. I hope you know how lucky it is to have you. I hope you learn that you are more than who your family has claimed you to be. You can break the generational trauma and prove them wrong. I hope you know that you're not a bad person for choose to distance yourself from the ones who have made you lose your sense of value in this world. I hope you know that it's okay to leave the place you were never able to call home in order to find it within yourself.

The way to healing yourself is not by only choosing the parts of you that you want to see. It's about embracing every inch of yourself forgiving the things you have done and what you have allowed yourself to endure. To fully, truly love yourself again, you must look into the eyes of your mind and let it show all of itself to you. You can't mend an injury without knowing the severity of the wound, thus you can't mentally heal without seeing yourself from all angles first.

It's hard to live in a time that doesn't suit you. How the things we're meant to care so much about mean little to you. The ways in which you must watch as the rest of the world is hypnotized to reality and slowly slipping away. It's hard to live in a world that has no heart. To never feel as though you belong. All you've ever wanted was to know what it's like to be missed, yet all you get are missed calls. It's hard to live in a world when you aren't meant to, and the loneliness that comes with is unbearable, isn't it? How aware you are of such a place, even yourself, and yet you're unable to get a word out to a gesturing hand. I know you can't see it just yet, but you will find an environment to settle down in. You will find the people to call your family. Even if it takes ages, you will know what it's like to feel loved and wanted in return; and I wish I could be there when that day comes. For your happiness is contagious, and you deserve to be excited about awaking each day. I know you will find what you're looking for, I just hope it isn't too far away from now. Though if it is, that's okay, because in the meantime you can focus on rekindling the love you had for yourself.

There's no right way to grieve someone, either dead or alive. The most common thing you get told is that, "time shall heal all wounds," but that isn't a sole conclusion to grief, at least not for everyone. If anything, you bottle up the feelings of sorrow along with the shock to make you think time has healed your wound, until everything comes out all at once. And that can stem from happing a day to even years later. We're so fixated on trying to "heal" and shy away from this pain we feel that we lose ourselves altogether. Grieving isn't about trying to forgetting them or what they meant to you. It's about honoring the moments you had with them and carrying on in life *for* them. It's about striving through and with those memories, being happy you got to spend and learn as much as you have about them while you could; because we never have enough time with each other. It's about crying, though not just out of yearning, but out of the love that you still carry out for the person you have lost, the love you could never fully express as it is infinite. Instead of wishing for the grief to go away, look at it as the remaining proof of how much you value this person, and the unexpressed love that you'll forever have.

In the moments when the one person who you never imagined living without has left you, it can feel as though you have been knocked all the way down to the very first step again. You feel as your world has been permanently fractured, and you don't know if you can survive its change. Let me remind you that you have had these exact thoughts before, and look at you now. Do not underestimate yourself, my darling friend. Do not think of yourself any lower just because someone made the mistake in trusting their luck with someone else. Perhaps you'll look back on today in a few years and be grateful they left. For you wouldn't have done it yourself, and it was their absence that provided you the space to grow.

When you meet the right person, they will look at you as though God has sent his finest angel to them. They will question what they have done to deserve someone like you. You won't ever have to doubt their love for you, they will shower you in it. They will offer their shoulder to lay your sword. They will sing you sonnets and compare your love to that of wings and the skies it airs, how you grace their boundless sky and inspire them to fly. They will kiss all of your bruises away, and tell you how that in which you wish to rid yourself from are all of the things about you that they couldn't live without.

If you're like me, someone who doesn't settle with small talk. Who prefers to bond through meaningful conversations rather than disputes of gossip. Someone that longs to find that in which beats the hearts of others. If you're someone who becomes inspired by the psyche of another, who gets drained quite easily when encompassed by confined minds: Never let the world force you to become another puppet for it to tame. Do not submit to the superficial tendencies that intoxicates the air we breathe. If refusing to orbit earth means to remain with just the company of yourself then let it be so. Disrupting your inner peace and lying to yourself to fit in and belong isn't worth it, let me assure you. Do not go against yourself just because the world envies your mind-drive.

Notice how trying to be a version of yourself that is being demanded by others is not possible. For it doesn't align with who you wish to be. Start to see how easier it is to be yourself than be who you're created to be in the minds of others. You genuinely can't live life and be liked by everyone, so why would you want to become a person that's being fantasized about by someone who doesn't appreciate who you are now? You get the luxury to change whatever you want about yourself. No one should have that much control over you to point where they can mold you in their image. Don't you ever give someone that much power over you.

This is your reminder that your productivity each day does not contribute to your worth. It's okay if you sleep in an extra hour. It's okay if you don't get everything on your list done. It's okay if you made plans for yourself and lose motivation the next day. It's okay if someone does more or less than you in a day. The only person you should compete and compare yourself to is who you were yesterday, no one else. Do not beat yourself up for taking a breather. Who you are and the reason people care about you is not merely about what you do. It's also about how you make them feel, it's about your passions and personality. If people choose to only care about you when you provide for them, it's not a genuine connection — just someone seeking parental-like needs due to not receiving it themselves. That has nothing to do with you, and it doesn't mean you can only be loved when invalidating yourself by supplying to others what you need yourself. Know that you're allowed to pause and breathe. Know that you don't have to define being wanted by your past experiences with incompetent people. Know that your worth is about more than just what you provide to others. Part of it is also about how you provide for yourself.

A Love's Soliloquy

This love that we share is draped by our hair

With summer's embrace of a golden light,
And winter's caress with its starry night
I would wage any war if you are peace,
My sword of despair smiling at your hope

And let it be known you are that of rain
As I undress my umbrella for you
For if I be bound to the needle's eye,
I shall seek the nectar that casts *your* eye

I loath midday for taking you away
As I'm lost at dusk on a stranded bay
Tell me, my love, is this to be our fate?
For if deemed so, I would like to escape

You are too eloquent to love afar,
Thus I shall wish upon a shooting star

To miss someone upon letting them go does not mean you have made the wrong choice. The truth of the matter is that it is through the feelings of hardship that bring the change that lifts you. Although you feel like this pain won't pass, and while you may think you can't hold up to your actions of removing them from your life, you can; and you will. Be patient with yourself, I promise you this wound will heal, it just takes time. You will wake one day and all of sudden see them as ordinary as you perceive yourself to be — though that's another thing to be worked on. These problems you face are of the clouds. They pop into our view for a few segments before migrating elsewhere. You are meant to feel every feeling in order to heal, so there's no need to fear it. You are going to be okay. You'll only become stronger from it, not weak for harnessing it.

You have no responsibility over how people react to you. The only thing that is in your control is how you act. If others choose to be upset with you, it is not your job to accommodate for it if they choose not to communicate it. They may think that how you make them feel is obvious, but that's not always the case. If they don't vocalize it and choose to grow resentful instead, things will only escalate without you ever knowing the reason to its full extent. There can't be comprehension without communication, even if you are good at reading people. So know that it is not on you for how people feel if they refuse to tell you, and the same applies to them. If you feel negatively about someone's words or actions, it is **your** job to communicate that to them in order for there to be a chance to exchange an understanding of both perspectives and resolve the issue at hand.

This is the illness we all share: The assumption of having time. We excuse our comfort in turning down opportunities because we think we'll be able to at another point. We hold off from pursuing what our hearts desire out of fear of being judged, rejected, or just failing. Let me remind you, and not to frighten you, but to open your eyes with the fact that our very existence has a time limit. Humanity, the simplicity of living, is a disease in itself. Eventually we will all pass away. While we may not know when that day is, we need to become aware that there will come a day where our last chapter is written. Where we watch our final sunset, drink our favorite beverage, where we collide hearts with the person we pledged to love in sickness and death. There's no escaping it, so why must you run away from the notion that we *don't* have as much time as you'd like to convince yourself of. It's time to start truly living, and not living through your fantasies as a way to tell yourself you can't achieve what it is that you wish to. Go out there and prove yourself wrong. Go out there and live the life you've dreamed of living.

Hollowed Truths

I look at the man who deems me unfit for him
And I see hollowed cords in his final breath,
Straining the words he wishes to say in his place
If only he knew how much we are the same
Our words slice our tongues more than our victims hearts
For we're believed that telling false truths will
Spare us from the hands of *Death* himself
Which is why I tell him it's okay
Though if I dare speak on my behalf,
I fear this day would be my last
And so I turn from him with a smile
My eyes welting a different tale

Meeting a Known Stranger

I have thought of such everyday,
Meeting you for the first time
Though I suppose I have just lied
For I have already met you
Perhaps not through the warmth of touch,
But of the heat of our synced hearts;
Of hearing your face through your teeth
See, the truth is I have met you long ago
For I know when your eyes light up,
Though I'm blinded of seeing your sight
I know the subtleties in each of your laughs
I know the places that inspire such joy in you,
Just as I know where to steer away from
So let me rephrase that;
When I say I have thought about meeting you for the first
time,
What I meant was that I can't wait to show you
The ways in which I love you,
The ways in which I have been limited to say
For you are no stranger to me,
But a voice I will see and learn to trace

Home in a Friend

You are what comes to mind when I think of home
For your arms are that of my walls,
As they encase me with safety
And your voice sings my clock each day,
Hushing me to bed when night awaits
Which makes your eyes its crown,
Getting lost in its beauty;
What I see upon awaking
Thus your smile is my 'sill,
Exhibiting hope of contagious purity
Therefore your legs are of the door to my chamber,
Anchoring my sorrows and shielding me of the beyond
Thank you for lending your keys when I'm in need
It means more than you know

When it's being said that the right person will find their way to you, make no mistake: You still need to put in the work to sustain your relationship with them. To have a genuine connection to another person, there has to be a balance of communication, willingness to learn, and understanding that who you choose to pursue a committed relationship with does not mean they symbolize all that life is. You need to make sure that you have a clear image of both who you are and also the kind of life you want. That way there's no imbalance of one accommodating the other way more than they should be. Your bondage with someone comes with responsibilities, both individually and harmoniously. You individually have to be in the right mental state to be able to differentiate your life with and without this person around you. You harmoniously have to continue to spend time together and build that intimate relationship that you wish to maintain. Your relationship with someone should be an add-on to your life, not the sole reason to why your existing.

Setting boundaries with people is not only about vocalizing what someone has done that goes against it. It's about enforcing action in response to those boundaries not being met if it has already been spoken about. Whether it's seeking reliable communication with someone that doesn't provide it even after you have told them, or if you seek a friendship with someone that's not just built on gossip and partying out, and yet they refuse to try and find a balance with you: You must withdraw in some form in order to solidify your feelings and consequence to when this boundary is not being met. Even though it may bring you ounces of guilt or the assumption that you're a bad person, you're not. It's you prioritizing the things you seek in others, and not dismissing it just because it's someone you love. It's keeping your word to yourself and retaining your values by not allowing the opposite into your life. This isn't to say that we should expect others to change for us, nor is it implying that people should. However, if someone cares about you enough, they will offer to openly discuss ways in which there can be a healthy balance of getting both needs met, just as you would for them.

To stop caring about what other people think is to no longer care about how you think other people are thinking of you.

Things exist for us to give them meaning. Just because you find something beautiful that another person does not, it doesn't change its value — for it has none, it merely exists. We get to decide for ourselves how much things mean to us, and not everyone will find what you enjoy to be favorable. And that's okay, people just look at it differently. This can be applied to who we are as well. If someone doesn't admire you, that doesn't change who you are, it simply means you aren't someone they connect with. Don't take someone's rejection so personally, and don't assume that there aren't people out there who can see your lovely aura. We exist among one another and gain our own preferences. What you love about yourself won't be for everyone, but don't use that as fuel to close your heart off from the ones who will.

A Eulogy of My Father

He planted a kiss on my forehead
And I could feel his salted saliva
As it moistures my skin;
He already tastes like death

The worst part about it was having
To accept that there was nothing I could do,
Apart from squeeze his hand blue
In hopes of regulating his heart

And when tranced in Sleeping Beauty's realm,
I found myself wasted among him
As I sat waiting for him to wake up;
Waiting for my chance to say goodbye

Though it never came,
So in turn, I picked up a pen and paper
And wrote him a letter
One I knew he heard through his wilted tears

And here I stand, nearly three years later,
Using poetry as my way to feel one with him
I know if he were looking down on me
He would be beyond proud of the person I have become

~ *I miss you, Daddio*

Baby Elephant Syndrome

I have always been latched to the bottom of the ocean,
Submerged by the world's commotion of its notion
The more I tugged in attempts to flea,
The further I sunk; 'till I could not longer see
When the tide surfs my lungs,
That's when I beg for an anchor the most
To hook me to the surface again
Though alas,
I have yet to reach Fishermen's coast
And I find myself growing scales and a tail
As the ocean-bed becomes my shore
When they finally find me,
I don't yank their chain
For I've sought refuge in my Titanic,
Deemed to believe this is to be my fate for eternity
Thus an offering hand raises, never seen again

Devoured Heart

My body has consumed my heart
More than anything else
And I should feel starved of a pulse,
Though I can't help but get high to
The feeling that it brings

When I stand, a hurricane awaits,
Its funhouse mirror reflecting my grave
And I savor the toxins' injections
For the only time I feel I am truly
Living is when I am scarce on life

And in turn,
I become the destroyer of keen
Trailing behind my maze of veins,
They who carve a manual to the cure
I dare not drink

~ *For I am the host of my own heart's malnourishment*

Haven is Not Such Without You

I had a dream where I found my haven,
A vibrant field of lilac skies
That had no dust of flies

And you stepped out of a tree trunk
With a hollowed smile,
As you extended your branch who sought out a leaf

The sun would kiss our cheeks in the morning
As the clouds would carry us to night,
Where the moon shined tales and the stars of chimes

Then at the brink of dawn,
We would give back to the early morning's dove
By exchanging our tender breath to one another,
Sending our love to the everlasting blues

Though now that I am awake,
I am still within our realm,
Yet without your fragrance;
Your stump sprouting your grave

And though it quivers the same serenity,
It is not worth gardening alone;
For I would rather divide Hell with you
Than be chained to Heaven's Gate

I gaslight myself into thinking I'm the flawed one, which pleads me guilty and has me stay with my "victim." And I know deep down that I'm not wrong, I guess part of me clings to the person that I've been told such stories about. The person I saw a fragment of long ago. Why do I crave those who can't give me what I seek? No matter how hard I try to convince myself otherwise, I settle for scraps on the bottom of shoes, and never trusting those who show me the littlest bit of kindness. Though perhaps it is time I face the truth, one that I've been in denial of and bargaining over: Being flawed is not what's at fault here. It's the fact that I see none in them which proves just how warped my perception really is

I want you to know that you are not an almost. You are not a maybe. You are not a possibility for the future. You are the guaranteed. You are a flat out yes. You are someone to be chosen now. I am truly sorry that you have been bent so much to the point of always expecting to be bruised. I am sorry people have worn you down and made you rusty, feeling stuck in the mold that they made for you to believe that you are nothing but to be used. I am sorry that you have never received the apology you dreamt of getting. I am sorry that life has not been the kindest to you, and that you have had to face it alone. But I am also proud of you. I am so proud of you for still being here battling life. I am proud of you for getting out of bed today. I am proud of you for finding motivation to still eat and hydrate yourself. I am proud of you for getting to this very page and reading it. I am proud of you for holding on despite it being hard. I am proud of you for wanting to better yourself and not be what you have been instilled you are. I am proud of you for allowing yourself to hear the opposite of what you have been telling yourself; that you are enough and worth loving and getting to know. And above all: I am proud of you for just trying, for that is all that should ever be asked of you.

My Oath to Death

Oh, *Death*,
How lovely you are
When looked afar our orbit
You are the just in this world
Who dares not discriminate,
And holds the proof that we are one
For when sentenced, there is no escape
There is no refuge found in Mother's arms,
There is no cure to conquer such curse
We simply pass on, our vined fate
Whether to the Devil or his beloved,
Another world or bound to an endless void,
Our souls become one with the earth at last;
And I find that absolutely beautiful
For you, my Reaper, you are the imitated,
Yet feared by those who capture you
You are ripe and spoken for,
Yet repented as if you are of sin
You are righteous,
And yet we are to look at you
As a means to an end
So when comes my time, my dear *Death*,
I shall pierce my heart for you
For no one knows the weight that you bear;
Not unless you have scathed yourself
By slaughtering those you once were
Though before that day,
I shall serve grateful to your existence
For you are the string which ties
Humanity as equal,
A knot that can never be untethered

There are other things in life that you can love that aren't another person. For instance, you can love watching sunrises and being one of the first people to start the day touched by the light. You can love the breakfasts you make. You can love a specific lyrics in a song in which you rewind over and over for. You can love a line from a poem that gets you to view its topic differently. You can love sinking in your bed after a long day at work, forgetting to shower and falling asleep. You can love when the school bell rings despite the, "the bell doesn't dismiss you, I do" speeches. You can love the smell outside after a storm. You can love the way your pet jumps up and scratches the door, tail wagging, when they sense you at the door. You can love to help people. You can love a specific city, country, capital. You can love to have the occasional splurge or cheat day. You can love journaling, writing diaries, poems, books. But most importantly, you can love yourself.

I may not visibly show it, but I am an incredibly sensitive person with abandonment issues. When I first meet someone, I tend to learn all of their mannerisms before anything else. So the smallest change in someone's tone of voice, their texting style, or even their body language can send me down this spiral of overthinking, amplifying what I already constantly fixate about. If someone cancels plans with me, even if the reason is absolutely valid, it's like the logical part of me empathizes and understands it, yet the emotional side of me, which takes more control, begins to use that as a conduit to start looking for reasons to why they canceled; and they are all targeted at me. If someone tells me they care about me, even though I crave those words more than anything, I pull away from them. I refuse to respond to their messages, their calls, and even avoid outings if I know they will be there. When I am meant to be productive, there are times where I physically daydream and act out conversations I wish to have with these people, getting lost in the notion of fiction from its reality. The reality that I wish for comfort, but deny myself from having based on the pattern of experiences with several people throughout my life. For the longest time I hated myself for doing this, always asking myself why I'm depressed over something *I'm* causing? But I realized it's my brain's way of protecting me. Based on factoring my relationship to other humans, my brain has analyzed that I have felt nothing but self-hatred and drainage from being around them, and so it protects me and itself from feeling that ever again. Which is why whenever I meet someone new I don't open up, nor do I stick around when I'm asked too much or am shown any appreciation. As much as I love myself for this, I need to learn that even though I have only been shown the opposite, there are places in this world where people would feel so grateful to know me. I need to learn that giving myself to the wrong people does not change the value of who and how truly lovable I am.

I hope you know that you don't have to be amidst a war zone for your feelings to matter. You don't have to question how valid they are. Your feelings are raw and genuine, and they deserve to be held with great care. Don't look at someone else's life and catastrophes and use them as a reason to deny yourself from being vulnerable. Don't disregard your pain because of the worst chapter of someone else's story. You are allowed to not be okay from time to time, no matter what the reason is. There is no wrong answer in feeling, for they are what show us the things that we care about the most. I want you to know that you aren't crazy for wishing physical harm on yourself in hopes to validate your inner turmoil. I understand how hard it is to try and prove you aren't okay when you don't have visible scars that exhibit it. That doesn't take away from its severity though, and that definitely doesn't change the way its causing you such hurt. I hope you learn to massage your wounds instead of patching it right away. I hope you learn to not be ashamed of your feelings, for there is no weakness in being delicate with yourself. I hope you learn that your feelings matter, and that you shouldn't run from them.

Echoes of Affection

The first time our lips touched,
It felt like words had finally been birthed;
Ones only my heart could beat into existence
And from that day forward,
I have thought of you ever since,
Droplets of you stirred in each part of my day
I think about the veins of our hands,
And how they create a Van Gogh painting
When pressed beside each other
I think about all of the poems I wrote for you,
The way each one was entangled with the truth
I think about how you loved me without saying such,
The way you stayed on the phone to
Make sure I got home,
Or how your thumb brushed mine
When my hand was on your chest
How your smile was an archway,
One that lead to the roots of my bliss
Or how you would wait for me in bed
To feel our harps strum in sync
Speaking love through silence was your specialty
And now that it's truly silent
I've grown to despise it
I want you to come home,
I want to return home again

It's rare to meet someone who you instantly become your truest self around. Someone who doesn't give you any reason to shy away from the world. Someone who inspires you to be the version of yourself you have always dreamed of becoming, yet never being able to believe you were capable of doing anything but dream. Someone who doesn't confuse you with how they feel. Someone who helps you relearn how it feels to be loved by another for simply existing, and not just for selfish reasons. Someone that challenges your taunting thoughts and quiets them. Someone that wakes up everyday and chooses you. Someone who respects your boundaries and doesn't gaslight you into getting what they want. Someone that contains a balance of humor and a genuine connection with you. Someone who accepts you for who you are, and who pledges to love all the versions of you now and to come. I hope you find someone like this, if you haven't already.

My Loved Skill

I haven't got talent in much,
Though what I can do is stamp my love
'Till the ink floods through my skin
I can write without ever straining my hands
I can wrap you in worded warmth which resembles a hug
I can cook you a meal, and should it burn,
I shall choose to eat it myself
I can sing amongst a woodpecker,
Fanning you with harmonious winds
That are whisked by my wings
I can make paper flowers,
And brand it with my blood to mark it a rose
I can bend my ribcage, the cell to my heart,
If needed a place to store yours for a while
I can be your shade,
The molten shedding thus upon me
I can be your exhaust,
Ushering you an extra mile forward
I haven't got talent in much,
Though I can love you without force,
For I would do anything if it meant
I get to have you in my life

You are more than just a wake for those who have chosen not to love you. You are more than the false promises you were kissed goodnight with. You are more than what has deemed you too uncanny for this world. Know that you will be okay. The scars that trace your skin and mind are badges, ones that signify the wars that you believed were worth fighting for once. These badges signify your triumph, for they have strengthened your armor; therefore the battle you're currently facing shall as well.

To miss them does not justify a reason for bringing someone back into your life upon letting them go. To miss them does not mean that you have made the wrong choice. To miss them does not contribute to your values. It's okay to feel hurt, and it's okay to want to rip open that band-aid just to hear their voice once more. However, you have to remember what outweighs the good that you seek, the good in which was not a permanent high to begin with. You don't miss them, you just miss the one thing that made you feel utterly happy and truly seen because you haven't found that in yourself yet. Which is why you have debated on the decision to let them go for so long, and why you still are. Hear me when I say it will get easier. The longer time goes on, the more opportunity you will have to seek for that comfort inward. It will take time to get out of the routine you made for them. You will have days where you subconsciously do things that you've always done for them. You will cry to songs that have brought you both joy. You will cook the meals they adored, even when you despised them. Though I promise you this, you will find others who will mend your tainted image on being loved. You will surround yourself with those who will sprout an even better routine, one that never leaves you questioning your place. It's not worth going back to someone who made you feel less of who you already don't know. Don't let this moment cause you to barricade yourself in protection from others. Don't let the mistreatment from one person justify all the reasons you have for not being enough and only worth letting go of when convenient.

To My Younger Self

I don't know who you are anymore
And I don't know what happened to you,
But seeing a picture of you smile
Brought more tears than I thought it would
I have lost you, and I am forever sorry
I'm left awake wondering where you ended up
Are you alone? Have you a family? Are you even here?
God, it kills me to wish you were here just to fix me
You should never have had to bear such at your age
Though I'd like to have gotten to know you more,
For I have no recollection of you
And from what I have seen,
You symbolized a reason to keep going
Thus I shall, little one,
Just for you

It's so often to see us find ourselves apologizing for being human, for supposedly asking for "too much." Allow me to remind you that you do not need to be sorry for wanting to be heard and respected. You do not need to be sorry for taking up space. You do not need to be sorry for wanting time to yourself. You do not need to be sorry for being hurt by someone else's actions, regardless of the intentions behind them. You do not need to be sorry for being excited about something that moves you. You do not need to be sorry for loving things the way that you do. You do not need to be sorry for wanting an apology. You do not need to be sorry for changing your mind. You do not need to be sorry for saying no and setting boundaries. You do not need to be sorry for falling out of love with someone. You do not need to be sorry for prioritizing yourself. You do not need to be sorry for letting go of those who don't wish to know you. You do not need to be sorry for anything but this; ever putting yourself in the position to believe that such things should be apologized for.

This is your reminder that even though you may judge yourself for the choices you have made and what you have done, you did what you thought was best at the time. We are not our faults, we are of our growth. Do not criticize a past version of you for the mistakes they made that have shaped you into the person you are today.

Perhaps the problem isn't about feeling better and getting past the pain that you have. Maybe the issue lies in trying to numb emotions that don't have the cause for them discovered yet.

I Am My Own Romeo

You look lovely in that dress, darling
I wish to see it frolic to my bedroom floor
So I can guide it to be washed and dried,
And wear it as a scarf for when your away

Your handwriting is exquisite, my love
I wish for your fingers to usher me
At the speed your pen does,
So I can finally know what it is to be Juliet

My, what lovely locks you have, honey
I wish to be draped by your hair on sunsets
So I can be guided through the night,
And scare the demons off with your light

Why, I look quite eloquent in a mirror,
Wouldn't you say?

I once went for a walk to clear my head from the chaos that I was amidst at home. I always take this lovely path along the train tracks because there's hardly anyone else there but me and the surroundings of nature. I'm not much of a crier, but I remember that day being a time where I had to let out everything that I was bottling up. It felt stupid at the time, but I turned to my right and saw one of the several trees eyeing me. I took out my headphones and walked up to it, and I found myself wrapping my arms around the giant. And I swear to you, I could feel it hug me back, causing the tears to finally flow and serve as my gift to the great oak; for being the first hug that I've had in too long. That was the day I looked at leafed creatures differently.

Become the version of yourself that **you** want to be. Don't confine yourself to the walls of other people's perceptions of you, for you'll never learn to grow that way. Don't fear the outcome you'll receive from those around you. If they choose to change due to you doing so then that proves just how much you have been settling for less. In becoming an authentic version of yourself comes the loss of people, even some you never thought would part ways with you. But that's the beautiful thing about growth, you will learn that it will be worth it. To be able to feel comfortable in who you are and surrounded by people who genuinely appreciate you compared to being what others want you to be and constantly wearing a facade, only being liked for the parts of you that they see themselves in. The reason they will leave once you loosen from their grip is because they won't recognize who's in front of them, and that will scare them. Those types of people seek control over situations, and at times that includes people. Know that it's okay for people to not accept you for who you are becoming. You are building a healthy relationship with yourself for once, so anyone who tries to jeopardize that just to keep you as you are is worth leaving behind. You'll begin to believe this with all of your heart once you start the journey of finding yourself. You are more than who others want you to be.

Stop fixating over the past and worrying about the future when you are spending no time in the now to contribute to either. The things that have occurred in the past are what have molded you to become the person you are today, and will used to determine who you wish to become — the future. The future is something that doesn't actually exist. There's no predicting it. Any choice you make can change your path. There is only the present. Focusing on each day as it comes rather than overthinking what may lie ahead will grant you the peace of mind you deserve. By staying with yourself today, you will help yourself for tomorrow.

Never regret the time you have spent with someone. Even if you have been hurt beyond measure, and even if you would be free of all of the troubles you now face if it weren't for them; we all come into each other's lives to teach ourselves lessons. While they may be harsh, they allow us to learn the most intricate things about what we long for. What we forbid ourselves to endure and what we crave. These hardships that you may grow through with others show you the chapters of yourself. From being strangers to wanting to know every inch of them to wishing you could forget them all together. A departing relationship of any kind is a collage of the ways you have shown love to another person, and in turn, how you both made each other feel at one point. While yes, you now regret your time together, in the moment you felt more happy than you were without them. We all make choices that we despise later down the line, but it is through that where we realize just how much our experience make us see clearer. It's not that we deserve to go through such things, it's a necessity in order to protect yourself from the modern world. It's a way to mold your heart to the things it deserves to desire. Though know that there is no limits for your heart, long for all that fills you with joy.

There is no end goal in finding who you are. The whole premise of living is constantly seeking out new things about yourself that will make life more exciting and adventurous. You will not have a day where you aren't becoming more than what you already are to the world.

Harmony Beyond Rhymes

I am not of a rhyming planet,
And I suppose it makes sense why
They're so drawn to me
For among these souls,
I find my home
Entangled of the same tapestry
The whistles of my heart,
Once loose and prosper,
Now caught on its last chord
And silenced by our own accord

Know that your feelings exist outside of the world of everyone else's feelings.

Just because you have no memory of enduring any forms of trauma does not give you a reason to invalidate yourself. There are times where the traumas you have aren't necessarily to do with what has struck you, but more so what didn't. If you're someone who is uncomfortable with physical touch, perhaps you never received such warmth like that from those around you growing up. If you refuse to talk about yourself in any capacity, perhaps you grew up without having a reliable emotional present family. If you find yourself hating silence and being alone, perhaps it's because there was nothing but chaos in your home and you learned to associate that with peace. Just because you have no memory of enduring any forms of trauma does not mean you haven't gone through any. Sometimes it's about the things that didn't occur that inflict the most harm on us.

Start doing things that make you uncomfortable. I'm not talking about the things that can place you in harmful situations. I'm talking about the things that you have stirred away from out of fear. The things that hold responsibility over the lowest days of your life. You find yourself forgetting the beats of your heart due to how you live in your mind more. I understand why it's hard to move forward, it's not easy to change your perception of something that has hurt you for so long. But I promise you, by facing them head on, you will be become comfortable in the things that make you uncomfortable. It's through doing the things you don't want to do that make you see that you're the most capable of reshaping your life from what has deteriorated it in the first place. You have the ability to paint the life you want to live, and you are more than able to relearn how to be okay with existing among the things that have taught otherwise. Just know that you can start whenever you want, and you don't have to do everything all at once; and you most certainly don't have to face them alone.

Ask yourself what has made you feel such a way about yourself, for at one point in time you saw yourself just as you do everyone else; a human being who's simply trying to navigate through the world around them. What has made you grown to believe that you trying isn't enough? I want you to notice the little things that you love about others and start looking at yourself with that same magnifying glass. I hope you learn to know that you're not doing anything wrong by existing on your own terms, and I want you to know that you can live life at your own pace.

There will always be a part of me that believes in the goodness of people. There will always be a part of me that believes love is not extinct. There will always be a part of me that will snuff out the cruelty of others in order to help heal them. Though I have been shunned for such beliefs, I have learned to be okay with that. For I empathize those who have grown up to fairytales being the source of their love rather than the very people who were meant to nurture them the same way.

The types of people you should allow into your life are those who are there for every potential version of you to exist. The ones who will hold you on your darkest days, celebrate with you on your accomplishments no matter how big or small, and laugh with you each day in between. The ones that give you a reason to keep going, the ones who make life a little more bearable. They are the ones that help you see all that was never wrong with you, and the things that you have blinded yourself from seeing in yourself. They are the ones who help you find your way back to yourself again without realizing it.

Tailored Vision

Oh, my dear,
If only you could pluck my eyes
And wear them for a while,
So you could see just how special
You truly are
For you use my seamstress' eyes
To button its quarrels away;
If only I could do the same for you

I hope through it all, you learn to be naked with yourself more than anyone else. I hope that you learn to hold yourself tight because you want to, not because there's no one else to hold. I hope that you choose to keep going for you, for the younger you that had dreams of conquering the world rather than being swallowed by it. I hope that you learn to be loud, to not fear yourself and question the importance of what you wish to say. I hope that you find the people that prove your mind wrong, that provide you with several reasons to why you are worth spending time on. I hope that you can forgive yourself without bruises. I hope that you find a passion that ignites such joy in you, and I hope for you to be satisfied with the life you are and will be living. I hope that you learn to not be so guarded with your heart. I hope that you will one day see yourself the way I see you. I hope that you learn just how much you truly do matter, and how different the world would be without you in it.

If the way you love others is filled with that which can only be dreamt of, imagine how much more beautiful it would be to finally learn to supply all of that back into yourself.

Comfort in The Discomfort of Drowning

I fear that it's just the idea of me that people adore,
And how the person I long to be is silenced by them
I long to be looked at and chosen to explore,
In hopes that insanity is not of my condemned
I fear that once they get to know me,
They'll begin to want to sculpt my image
Into the person I have yet to forgive for their torment

It has always frightened me,
How our days cannot be predicted
Like how our fire fades to graved sand,
And the grips of our love sink along the shore
I wish to be bathed in waves of wanting,
Strummed the reasons to why I am loved
Yet I hide from the touch of other's tongues,
Afraid that the ocean's salt got to them first

Destined to Detach

I reckon we were mended into the same soul
And were deemed too precious for this world,
Kneaded into what perfect would have looked like
Thus we were detached from birth,
Molded into two separate entities
That found their way back to each other anyway

When I first saw you again,
It was as if I could truly appreciate the air that we breathe
For the world has become more clearer with you in it,
And I find a dash of you in every part of my day,
Without you having to be beside me

I am glad that we weren't made as one,
For I would have no one to share such a life with,
Nor would I find joy in a world without you in it
I am glad that we exist alongside each other,
And I am glad that we orbit the parts of us that have been
Shunned by the outsiders who we must reside by

I am glad that we get to experience life
Through both of our lenses,
And I am proud to be someone who gets to
Wake up each day and know they have a person
Like you in their life

There's a version of us out there that didn't get to meet
And my heart goes out for them dearly

I have been instilled to believe that the farthest I can go stops at dreaming. I have never had the confidence to think I can achieve the things that I yearn for. It's hard growing up and being denied of wanting to be a princess. For when I now seek a passion of mine, my first thought is to fixate about it instead of fix the unhealthy relationship I have with myself when it comes to refusing to fight for the things I want to do in my life. It's a maddening type of illness, becoming sane from the insanity. Too self-aware about the things I think about, and too self-critical on the excuses that I turn into reasons for why I don't deserve to seek more. The truth of the matter is if it's something that's being played again and again within your mind, don't ignore it. Even though you don't think you deserve it, and even when you deny yourself of pursuing what excites you now, you will look back on it and be solely flooded with thoughts of what could of been. I know it's scary, but think about how much ease your mind will be at if you finally refuse its negativity by listening to what it's showing in a different way? What if rather than seeing all of the reasons to why you *can't* do it, you take that as motivation to go for it and prove yourself wrong; and in turn gaining some control back in your life? What if the answer has lied within you all along?

I find myself squeezing into spaces that are too tight for me and still expect to have room to breathe. I hide from who I am when around others, showing the truest parts of me only to myself. Sometimes we have to face near death in order to realize that forcing ourselves to belong in a place that doesn't see us is far more suffocating than waiting to meet those who will be allured by everything about us.

The Evolution of Drugs

Drugs used to be just pills,
Capsuled snow globes urging to corrupt
You would take them *only* when told to,
Not wanting to cause a storm

Yet here we are decades later,
With strips of yarned veins
Both woven and fragile,
And its needle piercing our strings to threads

Its labeled tins get tossed in the bin
As we seek to rid ourselves of dealing with living
Though no matter how much we try,
We're brought back to invest in the addiction it brings

We dry our eyes through the sponge of our phones
As they drain our lives before our very eyes;
All in hopes of numbing how we feel,
Never knowing when to stop

We don't reap what we sow anymore,
Having learnt to plant dye in other's tea
Out of fear of being poisoned first;
We have grown to be afraid of one another

This disease now spreads,
For our bodies bleed to get us to want more
And the high in which we crave costs us our hope,
As we seep into the depths of ourselves that cannot get out

~ *A hard pill to swallow*

<u>Apologies You Should Have Gotten</u>

I am sorry that my actions gave you a reason to believe that you don't belong anymore. I am sorry that my choice of words attest to why you no longer open up about how you feel. I am sorry that my neglect towards you made you fear people who want to know you in the way that I should have wanted to. I am sorry for being the perpetrator of why you think your voice isn't worth hearing. I am sorry for not being there when I promised to be. I am sorry for not believing you. I am sorry for disregarding how you feel just because you always told me you were okay. I am sorry for disappearing without explaining why and making you think you were the problem. I am sorry that I even did things to you that would make me need to be sorry.

You didn't deserve any of that, and there are no words that could make up for what I have inflicted on you. I should have been better to you instead of taking you for granted. I should have done more for you since you always prioritized me, even over yourself. I was in a dark place, and I used you to find a way back into the light, and that was wrong of me to abuse. Not many people, if any, get to have someone like you, and I am very sorry I took advantage of that with the knowledge I had. I know I can't change what's been done, but I do hope you'll allow me to be there and help you heal, just as you have always offered to me. I understand if you need more time and space from me, I just want you to know that I am sorry.

I am really **really** sorry.

Dear Reader,

Oh, I can see it now
The way you're scanning this home,
Its roof held up by your hands
Just the thought of you brings me such joy,
So I can only imagine what being in your
Presence would actually feel like

I wanted to thank you
Thank you for eyeing my journey,
For getting me to share who I am to the world
Thank you for taking the time to listen,
For taking a ride through my many stories
I hope that if you relate to me you felt seen

I hope that the words within these pages have
Helped you learn about yourself in the ways it has for me
I hope that you will pick up a pen and paper and grant
Yourself the voice that deserves to be heard
I hope that you have learned how invaluable you are,
And above all else, I hope that you learned you are never alone

- Cas

ABOUT THE AUTHOR

Cassandra Napoli is a 17 year old Italian-American poet. She wrote
her first debut poetry book as a reflection of her passion for
storytelling and a genuine desire to ignite the same fire in her
readers. With each verse, she hopes to inspire others to pick up a
pen and dive into the magic of expression. Her words are a beacon
of motivation, urging people to embrace self-improvement and
find solace in putting their thoughts and feelings on paper.
Through her heartfelt lines, she aims to create connections and be
a voice to the unsaid, letting others discover the bits of themselves
they didn't know they had, or have even been denied to say.

@cas.napoli on Instagram